T0007720

HOW TO FLOURISH

ANCIENT WISDOM FOR MODERN READERS

■ ■ ■ ■

HOW TO
FLOURISH

■ ■ ■ ■ ■

An Ancient Guide to Living Well

Aristotle

Selections from the *Nicomachean Ethics*

*Selected, translated, and introduced
by Susan Sauvé Meyer*

PRINCETON UNIVERSITY PRESS
PRINCETON AND OXFORD

Published by Princeton University Press
41 William Street, Princeton, New Jersey 08540
99 Banbury Road, Oxford OX2 6JX

press.princeton.edu

All Rights Reserved

ISBN 9780691238623
ISBN (e-book) 9780691238630

British Library Cataloging-in-Publication Data is available

Editorial: Rob Tempio and Chloe Coy
Production Editorial: Sara Lerner
Text Design: Pamela L. Schnitter
Jacket Design: Heather Hansen
Production: Erin Suydam
Publicity: Alyssa Sanford and Carmen Jimenez
Copyeditor: Kathleen Kageff

Jacket Credit: Statue of Aristotle by colaimages / Alamy Stock Photo

This book has been composed in Stempel Garamond

Printed on acid-free paper. ∞

Printed in the United States of America

1 3 5 7 9 10 8 6 4 2

This volume is dedicated to the memory of
Marie Crossen
(1934–2020)
who first taught me to love Greek

CONTENTS

ACKNOWLEDGMENTS

Many thanks to Rob Tempio of Princeton University Press for inviting me to undertake this project, which I have found immensely rewarding and enjoyable, one of the bright spots in the long months of the pandemic. Special thanks are also due to the *Thesauras Linguae Graecae* of the University of California Irvine for providing a digital copy of the Greek text that is printed in this volume.

Various drafts of the manuscript were discussed at online workshops at the University of Pennsylvania and at New York University during the fall semester of 2021. I am grateful for suggestions and corrections from Adam Beresford, Andrew Culbreth, Paula Gottlieb, Justin Humphries, Craig Knoche, Toomas Lott, Marko Malink, Phillip Mitsis, Jessica Moss,

Usha Nathan, Henry Newell, Andrew Payne, Brian Reese, Matthew Solomon, Franco Trivigno, Rosemary Twomey, Artur Vllahiu, Tamsin de Waal, Matt Walker, and Stephanie Wesson. Adam Beresford and Paula Gottlieb, as readers for the press, gave meticulous written comments on an earlier draft of the translation and were heroically patient in responding to my subsequent queries and proposals. Matt Walker was a cheerful sounding board during the final round of revisions. Any remaining errors are entirely my own, and I welcome hearing from readers who bring them to my attention.

JUNE 2022

INTRODUCTION

Athens in the fourth century BCE was the intellectual hub of the Greek-speaking world, attracting scholars from across the Mediterranean, many of whom came to work or study at Plato's Academy. One these was Aristotle, born in 384 BCE in the Greek kingdom of Macedon, where his father served as physician to the royal family. He arrived in Athens at the age of seventeen and remained a member of the Academy until the death of Plato twenty years later in 347. Aristotle then left Athens and spent several years in the eastern Aegean with other members of the Academy, returning to Macedon in 342 at the behest of King Philip. There he served as tutor to a young Alexander the Great. After returning to Athens in 335 he founded his own school, the Lyceum, and remained in

Athens until the death of Alexander twelve years later in 323. With anti-Macedonian sentiment on the rise in Athens, Aristotle left for the island of Euboia, where his mother's family owned property. He died within the year, at the age of sixty-two.

Aristotle's extensive writings ranged widely over topics such as logic, metaphysics, biology, poetics, rhetoric, ethics, and politics. The present volume contains an abridged version of his *Nicomachean Ethics*.

HAPPINESS AND FLOURISHING

For philosophers in the ethical tradition originating with Socrates and vividly depicted in the dialogues of Plato, the central question in ethics is "how should you live?" (Plato, *Gorgias* 492d). When Aristotle takes up this question in the *Nicomachean Ethics*, he formulates it as an inquiry into how to *live well*. Ancient Greek

has a term for living well: *eudaimonia*. So Aristotle construes his inquiry into living well as an inquiry into eudaimonia.

This crucial Greek term is usually rendered into English as "happiness"—although at the cost of potential confusion. By "happiness" speakers of English today tend to have in mind a feeling of contentment or pleasure. But for a Greek speaker of Aristotle's era, to attribute eudaimonia to a person is simply to say that their life is going well, without specifying what it is about the life that makes it a good one. Aristotle and his contemporaries debate whether pleasure is enough for eudaimonia, and later Greek philosophers will even dispute whether it is necessary.[1] So we need to translate *eudaimonia* in a way that makes the debate intelligible and does not give the false impression that theories identifying eudaimonia with pleasure are correct simply as a matter of semantics.

Some scholars try to avoid this confusion by translating *eudaimonia* as "flourishing." To say that someone is flourishing is indeed to say that they are doing well, not that they are feeling pleased or content. The concept of flourishing has undergone a renaissance of sorts in recent years, as philosophers, psychologists, and policy analysts seek a more appropriate and less reductive metric of human well-being than economic markers such as per capita GDP or medical markers such as the absence of disease. "Flourishing" is a good concept to invoke in these contexts since it suggests a more robust standard for well-being: fulfillment of potential, rather than the mere absence of pathology. Aristotle's own account of what makes a person *eudaimōn* would be quite accurately described as an account of human flourishing. We achieve eudaimonia, in his view, by fully realizing our potential as human beings. Most of Aristotle's ethical writing is devoted to identifying our many-faceted po-

tential, its basis in our nature, and the challenges we face in realizing it.

Still, I do not translate *eudaimonia* as "flourishing."

While I agree that Aristotle's ethics is indeed about human flourishing, I think "flourishing" better captures Aristotle's *answer* to the question—What is eudaimonia?—than it elucidates the question itself. Aristotle's inquiry is into the good life, and we should aim to translate *eudaimonia* in a way that preserves this crucial information. In older English usage, "happy" and "happiness" used to mean something very much like "doing well"—vestiges of which may still be discerned in such phrases as "a happy coincidence." In this older sense, "happy" is sometimes interchangeable with "blessed."[2] Consider the formula for the Beatitudes in the Sermon on the Mount, written in Greek some three centuries after Aristotle: "Blessed are the meek. . . . Blessed are the merciful. . . ." (Matthew 5:3–12). In the King James

version, "blessed" translates the Greek term *makarios*, which Aristotle uses as a near synonym of *eudaimōn* in the *Nicomachean Ethics*. You might describe the *Nicomachean Ethics* as a pagan version of the Beatitudes. Aristotle asks what makes a person happy or blessed, and he answers that a happy life is a flourishing one: a life in which we realize our full potential as rational, emotional, and social beings. While he insists that a flourishing life is our own doing, rather than a gift of the gods, he takes a theological perspective in the closing chapters of the work. In uncharacteristically elevated language, he states that people who lead flourishing lives are "exercising immortality" (*athanatizein*, 1177b33). They make the most of the godlike element in human nature and are "most beloved by the gods," who "rejoice in what is best and most akin to themselves" and "reward the people who cherish and honor it most highly" (1179a26–28).

Aristotle's Works

The works Aristotle published in his lifetime were praised in antiquity for their style but are almost entirely lost to us. The treatises that have come down to us, including the *Nicomachean Ethics*, were compiled more than two centuries after Aristotle's death by Andronicus of Rhodes, from writings that Aristotle left behind but had not prepared for publication.[3] These writings are famously terse, often crabbed in their style, and some scholars have speculated that they comprise lectures Aristotle delivered at the Lyceum, periodically updated and revised over the years. As a rough approximation, we may say that the organization into treatises, books, and chapters is the work of Andronicus, while the texts thus organized were written by Aristotle, or perhaps dictated by him, even if he did not intend us to read them in this form.

In the Aristotelian corpus as organized by Andronicus, there are two ethical treatises, the *Eudemian Ethics* and the *Nicomachean Ethics*. The latter is generally (although not universally) considered to be the later work, containing Aristotle's more developed views.

THIS VOLUME

In the selections from the *Nicomachean Ethics* translated in this volume, I have tried to stick to Aristotle's main claims and positive arguments, omitting digressions, repetitions, methodological remarks, and skirmishes with opponents, as well as many references and quotations that would have been familiar to his original audience but are less accessible to the modern reader. These omissions are marked by ellipses (...). Where a significant amount of text is omitted, I summarize it briefly in connecting comments, so that the reader can keep track of the overall shape and direction of the work.

The most severely abridged parts of Aristotle's text are the detailed treatment of justice in book 5 and the lengthy discussions of weakness of will, friendship, and pleasure that occupy books 7, 8, and 9 and the first half of book 10. I have pared those discussions down to the bare bones. What remain are the parts of the *Nicomachean Ethics* that I would normally assign to students studying Aristotle for the first time.

Aristotle sometimes uses concepts or vocabulary that requires an explanation. For example, he frequently invokes the soul and its virtues but construes these notions in ways that a modern reader might not expect. As an unobtrusive aid to the reader, the connecting comments briefly explain these and other key notions as they arise, and the graphics in the appendix summarize his conception of the soul and its virtues. The brief list of Aristotelian terms at the end of the volume will help readers locate those explanations.

My goal as a translator has been to render Aristotle's prose into ordinary English that is no more formal than Aristotle's own style. I have tried to avoid archaic constructions in English, even if these mirror Aristotle's own sentence structure. Where Aristotle makes a general statement with no definite subject, I translate with "they," "you," or "someone" rather than the overly formal "one." I have aimed for consistency in rendering key formulas that are crucial to Aristotle's exposition, but not at the cost of sacrificing intelligibility. Occasionally I will explain translation choices in the connecting comments or notes.

The Greek text that I translate was edited by Ingram Bywater (*Aristotelis Ethica Nicomachea.* Oxford: Clarendon, 1894); it is printed on facing pages. The few occasions where I have deviated from Bywater's text are marked by superscript in the Greek text and explained in the textual notes at the end of the volume. The Arabic numbers in square brackets—e.g.,

"[1.7]"—refer to book and chapter, respectively, as numbered in Bywater's edition. The other modern edition, by Franz Susemihl (Leipzig: Teubner, 1912), makes different chapter divisions in some places. It is customary to refer to specific passages in Aristotle's works by the page, column, and line numbers in Immanuel Bekker's Prussian Academy edition (Berlin, 1831)—for example, "1109a12." In the index of passages translated, I indicate the opening and closing Bekker lines for each passage. The titles and headings inserted into the translation and collected in the table of contents are my own contribution. They are intended to aid (or pique the interest of) the modern reader.

FURTHER EXPLORATION

The selections in this volume amount to approximately 25 percent of the text of the *Nicomachean Ethics*. Readers whose intellectual appetite is whetted by this bare-bones tour

and who would like to explore Aristotle's ethics more deeply are encouraged to read the work in its entirety. There is a wealth of excellent English translations to choose from, listed in the further reading section at the end of this volume.

HOW TO FLOURISH

[1.1] Πᾶσα τέχνη καὶ πᾶσα μέθοδος, ὁμοίως δὲ πρᾶξίς τε καὶ προαίρεσις, ἀγαθοῦ τινὸς ἐφίεσθαι δοκεῖ· διὸ καλῶς ἀπεφήναντο τἀγαθόν, οὗ πάντ' ἐφίεται. . . .

πολλῶν δὲ πράξεων οὐσῶν καὶ τεχνῶν καὶ ἐπιστημῶν πολλὰ γίνεται καὶ τὰ τέλη· ἰατρικῆς μὲν γὰρ ὑγίεια, ναυπηγικῆς δὲ πλοῖον, στρατηγικῆς

1. THE GOAL OF LIFE

(Book 1)

Aristotle opens his treatise by remarking that goal-directed activity is pervasive in human life. He extrapolates to the notion of a single goal or purpose for all of human life, which he calls "the good" or "the human good."

Human Pursuits

[1.1] Every art and every discipline, and likewise every action and every choice, seems to aim at some good. That is why people have rightly proposed *the good* to be what everything aims at. . . .

Since there are many different actions, arts, and sciences, there are also many goals. For example, health is the goal of medicine, a ship

δὲ νίκη, οἰκονομικῆς δὲ πλοῦτος. ὅσαι δ᾽ εἰσὶ τῶν τοιούτων ὑπὸ μίαν τινὰ δύναμιν, καθάπερ ὑπὸ τὴν ἱππικὴν χαλινοποιικὴ καὶ ὅσαι ἄλλαι τῶν ἱππικῶν ὀργάνων εἰσίν, αὕτη δὲ καὶ πᾶσα πολεμικὴ πρᾶξις ὑπὸ τὴν στρατηγικήν, κατὰ τὸν αὐτὸν δὴ τρόπον ἄλλαι ὑφ᾽ ἑτέρας· ἐν ἁπάσαις δὲ τὰ τῶν ἀρχιτε- κτονικῶν τέλη πάντων ἐστὶν αἱρετώτερα τῶν ὑπ᾽ αὐτά· τούτων γὰρ χάριν κἀκεῖνα διώκεται. . . .

[1.2] Εἰ δή τι τέλος ἐστὶ τῶν πρακτῶν ὃ δι᾽ αὑτὸ βουλόμεθα, τἆλλα δὲ διὰ τοῦτο, καὶ μὴ πάντα δι᾽ ἕτερον αἱρούμεθα (πρόεισι γὰρ οὕτω γ᾽ εἰς ἄπειρον, ὥστ᾽ εἶναι κενὴν καὶ ματαίαν τὴν ὄρεξιν), δῆλον ὡς τοῦτ᾽ ἂν εἴη τἀγαθὸν καὶ τὸ ἄριστον. ἆρ᾽ οὖν καὶ πρὸς τὸν βίον ἡ γνῶσις αὐτοῦ μεγάλην

is the goal of shipbuilding, victory is the goal of the general's art, and wealth is the goal of household economy. Where such practices fall under a single enterprise, in the way bridle making and the manufacture of other equipment for riding fall under horsemanship, and horsemanship itself and other practices of war fall under the general's art, and other practices in the same way fall under others—in all these cases the goals of the higher-up practices are more choiceworthy than those that fall under them, since the lower ones are pursued for their sake. . . .

[1.2] Now, if our actions have a goal that we wish for because of itself and we wish for everything else because of it (rather than always choosing because of some further thing, an infinite regress that would make desire empty and futile), clearly this goal would be *the good* and the best. Knowing it would surely have great impact on our lives, since we would be like

ἔχει ῥοπήν, καὶ καθάπερ τοξόται σκοπὸν ἔχοντες μᾶλλον ἂν τυγχάνοιμεν τοῦ δέοντος;

εἰ δ' οὕτω, πειρατέον τύπῳ γε περιλαβεῖν αὐτὸ τί ποτ' ἐστὶ καὶ τίνος τῶν ἐπιστημῶν ἢ δυνάμεων. δόξειε δ' ἂν τῆς κυριωτάτης καὶ μάλιστα ἀρχιτεκτονικῆς. τοιαύτη δ' ἡ πολιτικὴ φαίνεται· τίνας γὰρ εἶναι χρεὼν τῶν ἐπιστημῶν ἐν ταῖς πόλεσι, καὶ ποίας ἑκάστους μανθάνειν καὶ μέχρι τίνος, αὕτη διατάσσει· ὁρῶμεν δὲ καὶ τὰς ἐντιμοτάτας τῶν δυνάμεων ὑπὸ ταύτην οὔσας, οἷον στρατηγικὴν οἰκονομικὴν ῥητορικήν· χρωμένης δὲ ταύτης ταῖς λοιπαῖς [πρακτικαῖς] τῶν ἐπιστημῶν, ἔτι δὲ νομοθετούσης τί δεῖ πράττειν καὶ τίνων ἀπέχεσθαι, τὸ ταύτης τέλος περιέχοι ἂν τὰ τῶν ἄλλων, ὥστε τοῦτ' ἂν εἴη τἀνθρώπινον ἀγαθόν. εἰ γὰρ καὶ ταὐτόν ἐστιν ἑνὶ καὶ πόλει, μεῖζόν γε καὶ τελειότερον τὸ τῆς πόλεως φαίνεται καὶ λαβεῖν καὶ σῴζειν· ἀγαπητὸν μὲν γὰρ καὶ ἑνὶ μόνῳ, κάλλιον δὲ καὶ θειότερον ἔθνει καὶ πόλεσιν.

archers with a target and more likely to hit the mark.

If all this is so, we should try to grasp at least in outline what this goal is, and what discipline or capacity it belongs to. It would seem to belong to the most commanding and highest. The art of politics clearly has this status, since it determines which disciplines are needed in cities, who shall learn which ones, and how far. We see that the most honored capacities are subordinate to it: the arts of the general, of household economy, and of public speaking. Since politics employs all other disciplines and legislates what must be done and what not done, its goal would encompass the goals of the others and thus would be *the human good*. Even if it is the same for an individual and for a city, securing and preserving it for a city is a greater and more perfect achievement. While desirable for a single person, it is more splendid and godly for a nation and for cities.

ἡ μὲν οὖν μέθοδος τούτων ἐφίεται, πολιτική τις οὖσα.

[1.4] Λέγωμεν δ' ἀναλαβόντες, ἐπειδὴ πᾶσα γνῶσις καὶ προαίρεσις ἀγαθοῦ τινὸς ὀρέγεται, τί ἐστὶν οὗ λέγομεν τὴν πολιτικὴν ἐφίεσθαι καὶ τί τὸ πάντων ἀκρότατον τῶν πρακτῶν ἀγαθῶν. ὀνόματι μὲν οὖν σχεδὸν ὑπὸ τῶν πλείστων ὁμολογεῖται· τὴν γὰρ εὐδαιμονίαν καὶ οἱ πολλοὶ καὶ οἱ χαρίεντες λέγουσιν, τὸ δ' εὖ ζῆν καὶ τὸ εὖ πράττειν ταὐτὸν ὑπολαμβάνουσι τῷ εὐδαιμονεῖν· περὶ δὲ τῆς εὐδαιμονίας, τί ἐστιν, ἀμφισβητοῦσι καὶ οὐχ ὁμοίως οἱ πολλοὶ τοῖς σοφοῖς ἀποδιδόασιν. οἳ μὲν γὰρ τῶν ἐναργῶν τι καὶ φανερῶν, οἷον

These are the aims of our present inquiry, which belongs to the art of politics.

In chapter 3, Aristotle cautions his audience not to expect mathematical precision in this inquiry and warns that the topic is not suitable for the young.

THE PURSUIT OF HAPPINESS

[1.4] Let us resume our inquiry and ask: if every kind of knowledge and every deliberate course of action aims at some good, what good does the art of politics aim at? What is the highest good that we aim at in our actions? Well, there is general agreement on what to call it, since both ordinary people and sophisticated people say it is happiness, and they take living well and doing well to be the same as being happy. But most people disagree with learned people on how to specify what happiness is. To some it is a clear

ἡδονὴν ἢ πλοῦτον ἢ τιμήν, ἄλλοι δ᾽ ἄλλο—
πολλάκις δὲ καὶ ὁ αὐτὸς ἕτερον· νοσήσας μὲν
γὰρ ὑγίειαν, πενόμενος δὲ πλοῦτον· συνειδότες
δ᾽ ἑαυτοῖς ἄγνοιαν τοὺς μέγα τι καὶ ὑπὲρ αὑτοὺς
λέγοντας θαυμάζουσιν. ἔνιοι δ᾽ ᾤοντο παρὰ τὰ
πολλὰ ταῦτα ἀγαθὰ ἄλλο τι καθ᾽ αὑτὸ εἶναι, ὃ καὶ
τούτοις πᾶσιν αἴτιόν ἐστι τοῦ εἶναι ἀγαθά. . . .

[1.7] Πάλιν δ᾽ ἐπανέλθωμεν ἐπὶ τὸ ζητούμενον
ἀγαθόν, τί ποτ᾽ ἂν εἴη. φαίνεται μὲν γὰρ ἄλλο ἐν
ἄλλῃ πράξει καὶ τέχνῃ· ἄλλο γὰρ ἐν ἰατρικῇ καὶ
στρατηγικῇ καὶ ταῖς λοιπαῖς ὁμοίως. τί οὖν ἑκάστης τἀγαθόν; ἢ οὗ χάριν τὰ λοιπὰ πράττεται;
τοῦτο δ᾽ ἐν ἰατρικῇ μὲν ὑγίεια, ἐν στρατηγικῇ δὲ

and obvious thing like pleasure or wealth or honor. To others it is something else, in many cases a different thing on different occasions: health when they are ill, wealth when they are poor; when aware of their own ignorance, they are impressed by people who say it is something grand and beyond their grasp. Some have taken it to be other than and beyond this multitude of good things, something good in itself and the cause of those other things being good. . . .

For the rest of chapter 4, and in chapters 5 and 6, Aristotle discusses some of these alternative views, the last of which belongs to Plato.

[1.7] Turning back now to the good under investigation, what might it be? Clearly, it is different things in different practices and disciplines: one thing in the art of medicine, another thing in the art of the general, and similarly in all the rest. In any particular case, what is the good? Isn't it the point of the whole enterprise? That is, health in the case of medicine, victory

νίκη, ἐν οἰκοδομικῇ δ' οἰκία, ἐν ἄλλῳ δ' ἄλλο, ἐν ἁπάσῃ δὲ πράξει καὶ προαιρέσει τὸ τέλος· τούτου γὰρ ἕνεκα τὰ λοιπὰ πράττουσι πάντες. ὥστ' εἴ τι τῶν πρακτῶν ἁπάντων ἐστὶ τέλος, τοῦτ' ἂν εἴη τὸ πρακτὸν ἀγαθόν, εἰ δὲ πλείω, ταῦτα.

μεταβαίνων δὴ ὁ λόγος εἰς ταὐτὸν ἀφῖκται· τοῦτο δ' ἔτι μᾶλλον διασαφῆσαι πειρατέον.

ἐπεὶ δὲ πλείω φαίνεται τὰ τέλη, τούτων δ' αἱρούμεθά τινα δι' ἕτερον, οἷον πλοῦτον αὐλοὺς καὶ ὅλως τὰ ὄργανα, δῆλον ὡς οὐκ ἔστι πάντα τέλεια· τὸ δ' ἄριστον τέλειόν τι φαίνεται. ὥστ' εἰ μέν ἐστιν ἕν τι μόνον τέλειον, τοῦτ' ἂν εἴη τὸ

in the case of the general's art, a house in the case of the builder's art—different things in different contexts—but in any particular practice or project it is *the goal*, since everyone does everything else for its sake. So, if something is the goal of all our practice, it would be the *practical good*; and if there are several such goals, they would be the good.

We have now arrived at the same conclusion as before, but by a different route. Still, we should try to add more clarity.

Aristotle's next move is to introduce the notion of a "final" goal. The adjective he uses (TELEION) is translated "complete" or "perfect" in other contexts.

There are some things we choose because of something else, for example wealth, flutes, and instruments in general. So, although there are many goals, not all of them are final. Now, the best is evidently something final. So, if only one goal is final, it will be the good we seek, and if

ζητούμενον, εἰ δὲ πλείω, τὸ τελειότατον τούτων. τελειότερον δὲ λέγομεν τὸ καθ' αὑτὸ διωκτὸν τοῦ δι' ἕτερον καὶ τὸ μηδέποτε δι' ἄλλο αἱρετὸν τῶν <καὶ> καθ' αὑτὰ καὶ δι' αὑτὸ αἱρετῶν, καὶ ἁπλῶς δὴ τέλειον τὸ καθ' αὑτὸ αἱρετὸν ἀεὶ καὶ μηδέποτε δι' ἄλλο.

τοιοῦτον δ' ἡ εὐδαιμονία μάλιστ' εἶναι δοκεῖ· ταύτην γὰρ αἱρούμεθα ἀεὶ δι' αὑτὴν καὶ οὐδέποτε δι' ἄλλο, τιμὴν δὲ καὶ ἡδονὴν καὶ νοῦν καὶ πᾶσαν ἀρετὴν αἱρούμεθα μὲν καὶ δι' αὑτά (μηθενὸς γὰρ ἀποβαίνοντος ἑλοίμεθ' ἂν ἕκαστον αὐτῶν), αἱρούμεθα δὲ καὶ τῆς εὐδαιμονίας χάριν, διὰ τούτων ὑπολαμβάνοντες εὐδαιμονήσειν. τὴν δ' εὐδαιμονίαν οὐδεὶς αἱρεῖται τούτων χάριν, οὐδ' ὅλως δι' ἄλλο. . . .

several are final, the most final of them will be the good. In our view, a goal pursued for itself is more final than a goal pursued because of another thing, and what is never chosen because of something else is more final than the things chosen for themselves *and* because of it. We call *perfectly final* what is always chosen for itself and never because of another thing.

Happiness, it seems, is precisely this sort of thing. We choose it always because of itself, and never because of another thing. As for honor, pleasure, wisdom, and any virtue: we choose them both because of themselves (since we would take each of them even if nothing further came of it), but also for the sake of happiness, thinking that through them we will be happy. By contrast, no one chooses happiness for the sake of these things—or, for that matter, because of anything else. . . .

Aristotle gives further reasons for supposing that happiness is the human good, then argues for his

Ἀλλ᾽ ἴσως τὴν μὲν εὐδαιμονίαν τὸ ἄριστον λέγειν ὁμολογούμενόν τι φαίνεται, ποθεῖται δ᾽ ἐναργέστερον τί ἐστιν ἔτι λεχθῆναι. τάχα δὴ γένοιτ᾽ ἂν τοῦτ᾽, εἰ ληφθείη τὸ ἔργον τοῦ ἀνθρώπου. ὥσπερ γὰρ αὐλητῇ καὶ ἀγαλματοποιῷ καὶ παντὶ τεχνίτῃ, καὶ ὅλως ὧν ἔστιν ἔργον τι καὶ πρᾶξις, ἐν τῷ ἔργῳ

own conception of happiness in an argument that is sometimes called the "function" argument.

THE HUMAN FUNCTION

To find out what happiness is, Aristotle asks a famous question—what does a human being DO?—meaning, what sort of activity is characteristically human.[4] This question makes sense in light of the assumption in chapter 4 that happiness is the same as "doing well." If Aristotle can now identify what it is that humans DO, he can conclude that DOING IT WELL is what human happiness consists in.

[1.7, *continued*] While there is evidently general agreement that happiness is the best thing, we still need to state more clearly what it is. Presumably we might do this if we could grasp what a human being *does*. Consider a flute player, a sculptor, any artisan—in general, anything with a characteristic activity that it performs. Being good or doing well for such a

δοκεῖ τἀγαθὸν εἶναι καὶ τὸ εὖ, οὕτω δόξειεν ἂν καὶ ἀνθρώπῳ, εἴπερ ἔστι τι ἔργον αὐτοῦ. πότερον οὖν τέκτονος μὲν καὶ σκυτέως ἔστιν ἔργα τινὰ καὶ πράξεις, ἀνθρώπου δ᾽ οὐδέν ἐστιν, ἀλλ᾽ ἀργὸν πέφυκεν; ἢ καθάπερ ὀφθαλμοῦ καὶ χειρὸς καὶ ποδὸς καὶ ὅλως ἑκάστου τῶν μορίων φαίνεταί τι ἔργον, οὕτω καὶ ἀνθρώπου παρὰ πάντα ταῦτα θείη τις ἂν ἔργον τι; τί οὖν δὴ τοῦτ᾽ ἂν εἴη ποτέ;

τὸ μὲν γὰρ ζῆν κοινὸν εἶναι φαίνεται καὶ τοῖς φυτοῖς, ζητεῖται δὲ τὸ ἴδιον. ἀφοριστέον ἄρα τήν τε θρεπτικὴν καὶ τὴν αὐξητικὴν ζωήν. ἑπομένη δὲ αἰσθητική τις ἂν εἴη, φαίνεται δὲ καὶ αὐτὴ κοινὴ καὶ ἵππῳ καὶ βοῒ καὶ παντὶ ζῴῳ. λείπεται δὴ πρακτική τις τοῦ λόγον ἔχοντος· τούτου δὲ τὸ μὲν ὡς ἐπιπειθὲς λόγῳ, τὸ δ᾽ ὡς ἔχον καὶ διανοούμενον. . . .

thing will involve that activity, and the same will be true for a human being, if there is in fact a kind of activity characteristic of humans. Well, do a carpenter and a shoemaker each have a characteristic activity that they perform, but a human being has none? Are we naturally inactive? Or rather, since there is clearly an activity characteristic of the eye, and of the hand, and of the foot—and likewise for each of our parts—might we not likewise posit a kind of activity that belongs to us as humans, above and beyond all that? Well, what might that be?

Clearly, being alive is something we have in common with plants, but we are looking for something distinctively human, so we should set aside the life of nourishment and growth. Next would be the life of perception, but this too appears common to horse and ox and every animal. What's left is a life that employs our thinking part—one part of which is responsive to thought, while another part *has* thought and does the thinking. . . .

εἰ δ’ ἐστὶν ἔργον ἀνθρώπου ψυχῆς ἐνέργεια κατὰ λόγον ἢ μὴ ἄνευ λόγου, τὸ δ’ αὐτό φαμεν ἔργον εἶναι τῷ γένει τοῦδε καὶ τοῦδε σπουδαίου, ὥσπερ κιθαριστοῦ καὶ σπουδαίου κιθαριστοῦ, καὶ ἁπλῶς δὴ τοῦτ’ ἐπὶ πάντων, προστιθεμένης τῆς κατὰ τὴν ἀρετὴν ὑπεροχῆς πρὸς τὸ ἔργον· κιθαριστοῦ μὲν γὰρ κιθαρίζειν, σπουδαίου δὲ τὸ εὖ·

Aristotle's next move depends on the assumption that the kinds of life he has just enumerated are activities of the SOUL. *Soul, for him, is a biological and psychological principle; in plants it is the power of nutrition and growth; in animals it also includes the power of perception and locomotion; in human animals, it includes the additional power of thought. Human activity, for him, will be activity of the distinctively human part of the soul.*

So, let us suppose that characteristically human activity is activity of the soul: thinking activity, or activity connected to thinking. Now, what a thing characteristically does and what a good thing of its kind does are the same type of activity. For example, a kitharist and a good kitharist perform the same type of activity.[5] In all cases, the superior performance that comes from being good is *additional to* the activity. For example, a kitharist *plays the kithara*, while a good kitharists *plays the kithara well.*

εἰ δ' οὕτως, [ἀνθρώπου δὲ τίθεμεν ἔργον ζωήν τινα, ταύτην δὲ ψυχῆς ἐνέργειαν καὶ πράξεις μετὰ λόγου, σπουδαίου δ' ἀνδρὸς εὖ ταῦτα καὶ καλῶς, ἕκαστον δ' εὖ κατὰ τὴν οἰκείαν ἀρετὴν ἀποτελεῖται· εἰ δ' οὕτω,] τὸ ἀνθρώπινον ἀγαθὸν ψυχῆς ἐνέργεια γίνεται κατ' ἀρετήν, εἰ δὲ πλείους αἱ ἀρεταί, κατὰ τὴν ἀρίστην καὶ τελειοτάτην.

ἔτι δ' ἐν βίῳ τελείῳ. μία γὰρ χελιδὼν ἔαρ οὐ ποιεῖ, οὐδὲ μία ἡμέρα· οὕτω δὲ οὐδὲ μακάριον καὶ εὐδαίμονα μία ἡμέρα οὐδ' ὀλίγος χρόνος.

When Aristotle speaks above of "being good" he uses a single word, ARETĒ, *which will be translated "virtue" from now on. Although in English "virtue" is typically used for moral goodness,* ARETĒ *is a much wider notion for Aristotle and can refer to the goodness of anything.*

If all this is so—if we posit that it is characteristically human to live a particular kind of life, a life in which the soul is engaged in activities involving thought; that it is characteristic of a good person to do that well and finely; and that each thing is perfected by its own proper virtue—in that case, the human good turns out to be activity of the soul that comes from virtue. If there is more than one human virtue, the good will be activity that comes from the best and most complete virtue.

In addition, it must be in a complete life. One swallow doesn't make it spring, and a single day doesn't either, and similarly a single day won't make a person blessed and happy, and a short time won't either.

Περιγεγράφθω μὲν οὖν τἀγαθὸν ταύτῃ· . . .

[1.9] . . . εἰκότως οὖν οὔτε βοῦν οὔτε ἵππον οὔτε
ἄλλο τῶν ζῴων οὐδὲν εὔδαιμον λέγομεν· οὐδὲν
γὰρ αὐτῶν οἷόν τε κοινωνῆσαι τοιαύτης ἐνεργείας.
διὰ ταύτην δὲ τὴν αἰτίαν οὐδὲ παῖς εὐδαίμων ἐστίν·
οὔπω γὰρ πρακτικὸς τῶν τοιούτων διὰ τὴν ἡλι-
κίαν· οἱ δὲ λεγόμενοι διὰ τὴν ἐλπίδα μακαρίζον-
ται. δεῖ γάρ, ὥσπερ εἴπομεν, καὶ ἀρετῆς τελείας
καὶ βίου τελείου. πολλαὶ γὰρ μεταβολαὶ γίνονται
καὶ παντοῖαι τύχαι κατὰ τὸν βίον, καὶ ἐνδέχεται
τὸν μάλιστ᾽ εὐθηνοῦντα μεγάλαις συμφοραῖς
περιπεσεῖν ἐπὶ γήρως, καθάπερ ἐν τοῖς Τρωι-

Let this be our outline of *the good*. . . .

Over chapters 8–10, Aristotle shows that his out-line of the human good aligns well with what many people believe about happiness, and he considers what role good fortune plays in a happy life.

A FULL HUMAN LIFE

[1.9] . . . It makes sense that we don't attribute happiness to an ox or a horse, or any other animal, since they are incapable of engaging in the kind of actions that good people perform. For the same reason, children are not happy either, since they are not yet capable of performing those actions, because of their age. If we call them happy, it is on the expectation that they will be. After all, as we said, happiness requires both complete virtue and a complete life. There are many upheavals in life and all sorts of luck, and it is possible for someone living a thriving

κοῖς περὶ Πριάμου μυθεύεται· τὸν δὲ τοιαύταις χρησάμενον τύχαις καὶ τελευτήσαντα ἀθλίως οὐδεὶς εὐδαιμονίζει.

[1.10] Πότερον οὖν οὐδ᾽ ἄλλον οὐδένα ἀνθρώπων εὐδαιμονιστέον ἕως ἂν ζῇ, κατὰ Σόλωνα δὲ χρεὼν τέλος ὁρᾶν; εἰ δὲ δὴ καὶ θετέον οὕτως, ἆρά γε καὶ ἔστιν εὐδαίμων τότε ἐπειδὰν ἀποθάνῃ; ἢ τοῦτό γε παντελῶς ἄτοπον, ἄλλως τε καὶ τοῖς λέγουσιν ἡμῖν ἐνέργειάν τινα τὴν εὐδαιμονίαν; εἰ δὲ μὴ λέγομεν τὸν τεθνεῶτα εὐδαίμονα, μηδὲ Σόλων τοῦτο βούλεται, ἀλλ᾽ ὅτι τηνικαῦτα ἄν τις ἀσφαλῶς μακαρίσειεν ἄνθρωπον ὡς ἐκτὸς ἤδη τῶν κακῶν ὄντα καὶ τῶν δυστυχημάτων, ἔχει μὲν καὶ τοῦτ᾽ ἀμφισβήτησίν τινα· . . .

life to suffer terrible misfortunes in old age, like Priam in the stories about Troy. No one would call you happy if you experienced such misfortune and died so wretchedly.[6]

[1.10] Does that mean Solon[7] was right to say we must look to the end, and call no person happy while they are alive? If so, does that mean people are happy when they are dead? That would be strange, especially for those who say happiness is an activity! And if we don't call a dead person happy, and that is not what Solon meant—if his point is that only then can we safely declare a person happy, because they are outside the reach of evils and misfortunes—even that is open to dispute. . . .

After addressing these and other puzzles about happiness, Aristotle returns to his "outline" of happiness and clarifies the kind of virtue it involves.

[1.13] Ἐπεὶ δ᾽ ἐστὶν ἡ εὐδαιμονία ψυχῆς ἐνέργειά τις κατ᾽ ἀρετὴν τελείαν, περὶ ἀρετῆς ἐπισκεπτέον ἂν εἴη· τάχα γὰρ οὕτως ἂν βέλτιον καὶ περὶ τῆς εὐδαιμονίας θεωρήσαιμεν ... περὶ ἀρετῆς δὲ ἐπισκεπτέον ἀνθρωπίνης δῆλον ὅτι· καὶ γὰρ τἀγαθὸν ἀνθρώπινον ἐζητοῦμεν καὶ τὴν εὐδαιμονίαν ἀνθρωπίνην. ἀρετὴν δὲ λέγομεν ἀνθρωπίνην οὐ τὴν τοῦ σώματος ἀλλὰ τὴν τῆς ψυχῆς· καὶ τὴν εὐδαιμονίαν δὲ ψυχῆς ἐνέργειαν λέγομεν. ...

τὸ μὲν ἄλογον αὐτῆς εἶναι, τὸ δὲ λόγον ἔχον. ... τοῦ ἀλόγου δὲ τὸ μὲν ἔοικε κοινῷ καὶ φυτικῷ, λέγω δὲ τὸ αἴτιον τοῦ τρέφεσθαι καὶ αὔξεσθαι· ... ταύτης μὲν οὖν κοινή τις ἀρετὴ καὶ οὐκ

HUMAN NATURE AND HUMAN VIRTUE

[1.13] Since happiness is an activity of the soul that comes from complete virtue, we should investigate virtue. That way we might improve our thinking about happiness. . . . And it is clearly *human* virtue that we must investigate, since it is the human good and human happiness that we have been investigating. In our view, *human* virtue is not of the body but of the soul. Happiness, we say, is an activity of the soul. . . .

Thus we need knowledge of the soul, Aristotle notes, but not specialized expertise. We can get by, he says, with the account of the soul in his (now lost) popular writings, which he summarizes as follows.

Our soul has an unthinking part and a thinking part. . . . We share one aspect of the unthinking part with plants; it is the cause of nourishment and growth. . . . The virtue of this power is

ἀνθρωπίνη φαίνεται· δοκεῖ γὰρ ἐν τοῖς ὕπνοις ἐνεργεῖν μάλιστα τὸ μόριον τοῦτο καὶ ἡ δύναμις αὕτη, ὁ δ᾽ ἀγαθὸς καὶ κακὸς ἥκιστα διάδηλοι καθ᾽ ὕπνον . . .

ἀλλὰ περὶ μὲν τούτων ἅλις, καὶ τὸ θρεπτικὸν ἐατέον, ἐπειδὴ τῆς ἀνθρωπικῆς ἀρετῆς ἄμοιρον πέφυκεν. ἔοικε δὲ καὶ ἄλλη τις φύσις τῆς ψυχῆς ἄλογος εἶναι, μετέχουσα μέντοι πῃ λόγου. τοῦ γὰρ ἐγκρατοῦς καὶ ἀκρατοῦς τὸν λόγον καὶ τῆς ψυχῆς τὸ λόγον ἔχον ἐπαινοῦμεν· ὀρθῶς γὰρ καὶ ἐπὶ τὰ βέλτιστα παρακαλεῖ· φαίνεται δ᾽ ἐν αὐτοῖς καὶ ἄλλο τι παρὰ τὸν λόγον πεφυκός, ὃ μάχεται καὶ ἀντιτείνει τῷ λόγῳ. ἀτεχνῶς γὰρ καθάπερ τὰ παραλελυμένα τοῦ σώματος μόρια εἰς τὰ δεξιὰ προαιρουμένων κινῆσαι τοὐναντίον εἰς τὰ ἀριστερὰ παραφέρεται, καὶ ἐπὶ τῆς ψυχῆς οὕτως· ἐπὶ τἀναντία γὰρ αἱ ὁρμαὶ τῶν ἀκρατῶν. ἀλλ᾽ ἐν τοῖς σώμασι μὲν ὁρῶμεν τὸ παραφερόμενον, ἐπὶ

clearly common rather than human. Indeed, this part and power is at work primarily during sleep, when the difference between good and bad people is least discernible. . . .

But enough about the nutritive soul; let us set it aside, since by its nature it has no part in human virtue. Now, a different part of our soul's nature is also unthinking but nonetheless shares in thought in a way. Consider, for example, someone exercising self-control, or losing control. We praise their thinking—that is, the thinking part of their soul—because it correctly urges them toward the best course of action. But their nature clearly also contains something else alongside thinking that fights and pulls against it. What happens in their soul is very much like what happens in a body when a paralyzed limb moves in the wrong direction (for example, the limb moves left when you try to move it to the right). That is, people who lose control are pulled in two directions, even though we don't actually see the soul part moving in the wrong

δὲ τῆς ψυχῆς οὐχ ὁρῶμεν. ἴσως δ' οὐδὲν ἧττον καὶ ἐν τῇ ψυχῇ νομιστέον εἶναί τι παρὰ τὸν λόγον, ἐναντιούμενον τούτῳ καὶ ἀντιβαῖνον. πῶς δ' ἕτερον, οὐδὲν διαφέρει.

λόγου δὲ καὶ τοῦτο φαίνεται μετέχειν, ὥσπερ εἴπομεν· πειθαρχεῖ γοῦν τῷ λόγῳ—τὸ τοῦ ἐγκρατοῦς ἔτι δ' ἴσως εὐηκοώτερόν ἐστι τὸ τοῦ σώφρονος καὶ ἀνδρείου· πάντα γὰρ ὁμοφωνεῖ τῷ λόγῳ. φαίνεται δὴ καὶ τὸ ἄλογον διττόν. τὸ μὲν γὰρ φυτικὸν οὐδαμῶς κοινωνεῖ λόγου, τὸ δ' ἐπιθυμητικὸν καὶ ὅλως ὀρεκτικὸν μετέχει πως, ᾗ κατήκοόν ἐστιν αὐτοῦ καὶ πειθαρχικόν· οὕτω δὴ καὶ τοῦ πατρὸς καὶ τῶν φίλων φαμὲν ἔχειν λόγον, καὶ οὐχ ὥσπερ τῶν μαθηματικῶν. ὅτι δὲ πείθεταί πως ὑπὸ λόγου τὸ ἄλογον, μηνύει καὶ ἡ νουθέτησις καὶ πᾶσα ἐπιτίμησίς τε καὶ παράκλησις. εἰ δὲ

direction as we do in the case of the body. Still, an equally good case can be made about their soul: we should recognize in it something alongside thought that opposes and resists it. Exactly how it differs from thought is not important.

As we said, this element too seems to share in thought. When you exercise self-control, it is ruled by thought. If you have self-discipline[8] or courage, it is presumably even more obedient and agrees with thought about everything. The unthinking part of our soul is therefore clearly twofold: the plantlike element has nothing in common with thought, while the seat of appetites and desires shares in thought in a way—to the extent that it can heed and be ruled by thought, in the way you follow the advice of your father and friends (which is different from following a proof in mathematics). Admonition, chastisement, and exhortation are all evidence that our unthinking element is receptive to thought in some way or another. If it too must be called a thinking part, then our thinking part

χρὴ καὶ τοῦτο φάναι λόγον ἔχειν, διττὸν ἔσται καὶ τὸ λόγον ἔχον, τὸ μὲν κυρίως καὶ ἐν αὑτῷ, τὸ δ' ὥσπερ τοῦ πατρὸς ἀκουστικόν τι.

διορίζεται δὲ καὶ ἡ ἀρετὴ κατὰ τὴν διαφορὰν ταύτην· λέγομεν γὰρ αὐτῶν τὰς μὲν διανοητικὰς τὰς δὲ ἠθικάς, σοφίαν μὲν καὶ σύνεσιν καὶ φρόνη-σιν διανοητικάς, ἐλευθεριότητα δὲ καὶ σωφρο-σύνην ἠθικάς. λέγοντες γὰρ περὶ τοῦ ἤθους οὐ λέγομεν ὅτι σοφὸς ἢ συνετὸς ἀλλ' ὅτι πρᾶος ἢ σώφρων· ἐπαινοῦμεν δὲ καὶ τὸν σοφὸν κατὰ τὴν ἕξιν· τῶν ἕξεων δὲ τὰς ἐπαινετὰς ἀρετὰς λέγομεν.

will also be twofold: one element of it will be "thinking" in the strict sense of having thought inside it, while the other will be able to listen to thought, as to a father.

Virtue, too, can be divided along these lines. We call some virtues *virtues of intellect*, and others *virtues of character*. Being learned or discerning or having good judgment are virtues of intellect, while generosity and self-discipline are virtues of character. When speaking of character, we don't call someone learned or discerning; we call them even tempered or self-disciplined. But we do praise learned people for their disposition, and we call a praiseworthy disposition a virtue.

[2.1] Διττῆς δὴ τῆς ἀρετῆς οὔσης, τῆς μὲν διανο-
ητικῆς τῆς δὲ ἠθικῆς, ἡ μὲν διανοητικὴ τὸ πλεῖον
ἐκ διδασκαλίας ἔχει καὶ τὴν γένεσιν καὶ τὴν αὔξη-
σιν, διόπερ ἐμπειρίας δεῖται καὶ χρόνου, ἡ δ' ἠθικὴ
ἐξ ἔθους περιγίνεται, ὅθεν καὶ τοὔνομα ἔσχηκε
μικρὸν παρεκκλῖνον ἀπὸ τοῦ ἔθους.

ἐξ οὗ καὶ δῆλον ὅτι οὐδεμία τῶν ἠθικῶν ἀρετῶν
φύσει ἡμῖν ἐγγίνεται· οὐθὲν γὰρ τῶν φύσει ὄντων

2. BUILDING CHARACTER

(Book 2)
Aristotle now embarks on an extended discussion of the virtues of character.

LEARNING BY DOING

[2.1] Now virtue comes in two forms, virtue of intellect and virtue of character. The intellectual kind arises and grows from instruction, which is why it requires experience and time. Virtue of character, on the other hand, results from our regular practice [*ethos*]—which is why our term for character [*ēthos*] is a slight modification of "ethos."

It also clearly follows that none of the virtues of character develops in us by nature, since practicing won't train anything out of being what it

ἄλλως ἐθίζεται, οἷον ὁ λίθος φύσει κάτω φερό-
μενος οὐκ ἂν ἐθισθείη ἄνω φέρεσθαι, οὐδ' ἂν μυ-
ριάκις αὐτὸν ἐθίζῃ τις ἄνω ῥιπτῶν, οὐδὲ τὸ πῦρ
κάτω, οὐδ' ἄλλο οὐδὲν τῶν ἄλλως πεφυκότων
ἄλλως ἂν ἐθισθείη. οὔτ' ἄρα φύσει οὔτε παρὰ
φύσιν ἐγγίνονται αἱ ἀρεταί, ἀλλὰ πεφυκόσι μὲν
ἡμῖν δέξασθαι αὐτάς, τελειουμένοις δὲ διὰ τοῦ
ἔθους.

. . . οἷον οἰκοδομοῦντες οἰκοδόμοι γίνονται καὶ
κιθαρίζοντες κιθαρισταί· οὕτω δὴ καὶ τὰ μὲν
δίκαια πράττοντες δίκαιοι γινόμεθα, τὰ δὲ σώφρονα σώφρονες, τὰ δ' ἀνδρεῖα ἀνδρεῖοι. μαρ-
τυρεῖ δὲ καὶ τὸ γινόμενον ἐν ταῖς πόλεσιν· οἱ
γὰρ νομοθέται τοὺς πολίτας ἐθίζοντες ποιοῦσιν
ἀγαθούς, καὶ τὸ μὲν βούλημα παντὸς νομο-
θέτου τοῦτ' ἐστίν, ὅσοι δὲ μὴ εὖ αὐτὸ ποιοῦσιν
ἁμαρτάνουσιν . . .

naturally is. A stone, for example, naturally travels downward and could never be trained to travel upward, even if you practiced throwing it upward a thousand times; and fire cannot be trained to travel downward. The same goes for anything else that is naturally a certain way; it cannot be trained to do otherwise. So the virtues don't develop in us by nature, and they are not contrary to our nature either. We are naturally open to acquiring them, but it is by practicing that we reach our full development.

. . . For example, we become house builders by building houses, and kitharists by playing the kithara. Similarly, by doing justice we become just, by acting with discipline we develop self-discipline, and by performing brave acts we develop bravery. As a sign of this, consider what happens at the civic level, where lawgivers make citizens good by getting them used to acting in certain ways. Any lawgiver intends to do this, and any who fail to do it well are bungling the job. . . .

ἔτι ἐκ τῶν αὐτῶν καὶ διὰ τῶν αὐτῶν καὶ γίνεται πᾶσα ἀρετὴ καὶ φθείρεται, ὁμοίως δὲ καὶ
τέχνη· ἐκ γὰρ τοῦ κιθαρίζειν καὶ οἱ ἀγαθοὶ καὶ
κακοὶ γίνονται κιθαρισταί. ἀνάλογον δὲ καὶ οἰκοδόμοι καὶ οἱ λοιποὶ πάντες· ἐκ μὲν γὰρ τοῦ εὖ
οἰκοδομεῖν ἀγαθοὶ οἰκοδόμοι ἔσονται, ἐκ δὲ τοῦ
κακῶς κακοί. . . . οὕτω δὴ καὶ ἐπὶ τῶν ἀρετῶν
ἔχει· πράττοντες γὰρ τὰ ἐν τοῖς συναλλάγμασι
τοῖς πρὸς τοὺς ἀνθρώπους γινόμεθα οἳ μὲν δίκαιοι
οἳ δὲ ἄδικοι, πράττοντες δὲ τὰ ἐν τοῖς δεινοῖς καὶ
ἐθιζόμενοι φοβεῖσθαι ἢ θαρρεῖν οἳ μὲν ἀνδρεῖοι
οἳ δὲ δειλοί. ὁμοίως δὲ καὶ τὰ περὶ τὰς ἐπιθυμίας
ἔχει καὶ τὰ περὶ τὰς ὀργάς· οἳ μὲν γὰρ σώφρονες
καὶ πρᾶοι γίνονται, οἳ δ' ἀκόλαστοι καὶ ὀργίλοι,
οἳ μὲν ἐκ τοῦ οὑτωσὶ ἐν αὐτοῖς ἀναστρέφεσθαι,
οἳ δὲ ἐκ τοῦ οὑτωσί.

καὶ ἑνὶ δὴ λόγῳ ἐκ τῶν ὁμοίων ἐνεργειῶν αἱ
ἕξεις γίνονται. διὸ δεῖ τὰς ἐνεργείας ποιὰς

Virtue is *destroyed* through the same activities by which we acquire it, and the same is true for practical skills. People become both good and bad kitharists from playing the kithara, and similarly for house builders and all the rest. It is from building *well* that people become good house builders, and from building *badly* that they become bad ones. . . . The same goes for the virtues. From our transactions with others, for example, some of us become just, and others unjust. From the way we act in frightening situations, as we get used to feeling fear or confidence, some of us become brave while others become cowards. So too in matters of appetites and anger, some people develop self-discipline and an even temper, while others become self-indulgent and hot tempered— depending on how they conduct themselves in those situations.

In short, our dispositions will be of the same sort as the activities from which they develop. Our activities therefore need to be of the right

ἀποδιδόναι· κατὰ γὰρ τὰς τούτων διαφορὰς ἀκολουθοῦσιν αἱ ἕξεις. οὐ μικρὸν οὖν διαφέρει τὸ οὕτως ἢ οὕτως εὐθὺς ἐκ νέων ἐθίζεσθαι, ἀλλὰ πάμπολυ, μᾶλλον δὲ τὸ πᾶν.

[2.2] Ἐπεὶ οὖν ἡ παροῦσα πραγματεία οὐ θεωρίας ἕνεκά ἐστιν ὥσπερ αἱ ἄλλαι (οὐ γὰρ ἵνα εἰδῶμεν τί ἐστιν ἡ ἀρετὴ σκεπτόμεθα, ἀλλ' ἵν' ἀγαθοὶ γενώμεθα, ἐπεὶ οὐδὲν ἂν ἦν ὄφελος αὐτῆς), ἀναγκαῖον ἐπισκέψασθαι τὰ περὶ τὰς πράξεις, πῶς πρακτέον αὐτάς· αὗται γάρ εἰσι κύριαι καὶ τοῦ ποιὰς γενέσθαι τὰς ἕξεις, καθάπερ εἰρήκαμεν. τὸ μὲν οὖν κατὰ τὸν ὀρθὸν λόγον πράττειν κοινὸν καὶ ὑποκείσθω. ῥηθήσεται δ' ὕστερον περὶ αὐτοῦ, καὶ τί ἐστιν ὁ ὀρθὸς λόγος, καὶ πῶς ἔχει πρὸς τὰς ἄλλας ἀρετάς. . . .

sort, since the caliber of the dispositions will depend on the activities. That is why it makes no small difference how we get used to acting from an early age. Indeed, it makes all the difference in the world.

[2.2] Now, our present undertaking differs from others in that its goal is not just to know. We don't inquire in order to determine what virtue is, but to become good ourselves. Otherwise, there would be no benefit to it. Therefore, it is necessary to investigate actions—*how* we should act. It is necessary because, as we said, our actions determine what sort of dispositions we develop. Let us stipulate, as a common feature, that our actions should follow correct thinking. We will have more to say later about what correct thinking is, and how it relates to the other virtues. . . .

After warning us (again) not to expect too much precision from his remarks Aristotle resumes his account of virtue of character.

πρῶτον οὖν τοῦτο θεωρητέον, ὅτι τὰ τοιαῦτα
πέφυκεν ὑπ' ἐνδείας καὶ ὑπερβολῆς φθείρεσθαι,
(δεῖ γὰρ ὑπὲρ τῶν ἀφανῶν τοῖς φανεροῖς μαρτυ-
ρίοις χρῆσθαι) ὥσπερ ἐπὶ τῆς ἰσχύος καὶ τῆς ὑγιείας ὁρῶμεν· τά τε γὰρ ὑπερβάλλοντα γυμνάσια
καὶ τὰ ἐλλείποντα φθείρει τὴν ἰσχύν, ὁμοίως δὲ καὶ
τὰ ποτὰ καὶ τὰ σιτία πλείω καὶ ἐλάττω γινόμενα
φθείρει τὴν ὑγίειαν, τὰ δὲ σύμμετρα καὶ ποιεῖ καὶ
αὔξει καὶ σῴζει. οὕτως οὖν καὶ ἐπὶ σωφροσύνης
καὶ ἀνδρείας ἔχει καὶ τῶν ἄλλων ἀρετῶν. ὅ τε
γὰρ πάντα φεύγων καὶ φοβούμενος καὶ μηδὲν
ὑπομένων δειλὸς γίνεται, ὅ τε μηδὲν ὅλως φοβούμενος ἀλλὰ πρὸς πάντα βαδίζων θρασύς·
ὁμοίως δὲ καὶ ὁ μὲν πάσης ἡδονῆς ἀπολαύων καὶ
μηδεμιᾶς ἀπεχόμενος ἀκόλαστος, ὁ δὲ πᾶσαν
φεύγων, ὥσπερ οἱ ἄγροικοι, ἀναίσθητός τις·
φθείρεται δὴ σωφροσύνη καὶ ἡ ἀνδρεία ὑπὸ τῆς
ὑπερβολῆς καὶ τῆς ἐλλείψεως, ὑπὸ δὲ τῆς μεσότη-
τος σῴζεται.

The first point to note is that we are dealing with qualities that are destroyed by excess and deficiency—an abstract point we may support with some obvious examples. We see it happen in the case of strength and health. Exercising too much or too little destroys our strength, and likewise too much or too little food and drink ruins our health. Striking a middle course, however, produces, increases, and maintains these qualities. Exactly the same thing happens in the case of self-discipline, bravery, and the other virtues. For example, someone who flees and fears everything and endures nothing becomes a coward, while someone who fears nothing and goes to meet every danger becomes rash. Similarly, someone who indulges in every pleasure and refrains from none becomes self-indulgent, while someone who avoids all pleasures, like boors do, becomes impassive. So, self-discipline and bravery are destroyed by excess and deficiency, while taking a middle course preserves them.

ἀλλ' οὐ μόνον αἱ γενέσεις καὶ αὐξήσεις καὶ αἱ φθοραὶ ἐκ τῶν αὐτῶν καὶ ὑπὸ τῶν αὐτῶν γίνονται, ἀλλὰ καὶ αἱ ἐνέργειαι ἐν τοῖς αὐτοῖς ἔσονται· καὶ γὰρ ἐπὶ τῶν ἄλλων τῶν φανερωτέρων οὕτως ἔχει, οἷον ἐπὶ τῆς ἰσχύος· γίνεται γὰρ ἐκ τοῦ πολλὴν τροφὴν λαμβάνειν καὶ πολλοὺς πόνους ὑπομένειν, καὶ μάλιστα ἂν δύναιτ' αὐτὰ ποιεῖν ὁ ἰσχυρός. οὕτω δ' ἔχει καὶ ἐπὶ τῶν ἀρετῶν· ἔκ τε γὰρ τοῦ ἀπέχεσθαι τῶν ἡδονῶν γινόμεθα σώφρονες, καὶ γενόμενοι μάλιστα δυνάμεθα ἀπέχεσθαι αὐτῶν· ὁμοίως δὲ καὶ ἐπὶ τῆς ἀνδρείας· ἐθιζόμενοι γὰρ καταφρονεῖν τῶν φοβερῶν καὶ ὑπομένειν αὐτὰ γινόμεθα ἀνδρεῖοι, καὶ γενόμενοι μάλιστα δυνησόμεθα ὑπομένειν τὰ φοβερά.

[2.3] Σημεῖον δὲ δεῖ ποιεῖσθαι τῶν ἕξεων τὴν ἐπιγινομένην ἡδονὴν ἢ λύπην τοῖς ἔργοις· ὁ μὲν γὰρ

Another point is that when we *exercise* the virtues, we perform the same kind of actions as produce, increase, and even destroy them. That's the way it is in other very obvious examples, such as strength, which comes from eating a heavy diet and doing a lot of strenuous exercise. These are the very activities that a strong person is especially able to perform. It is the same with the virtues. For example, by refraining from pleasures we develop self-discipline, and once we have developed it, we are especially able to refrain from them. Bravery is the same. We become brave by getting used to making little of the things that frighten us and enduring them, and once we have become brave we are especially able to endure frightening things.

Feelings and Actions

[2.3] We should take the pleasure or pain accompanying our actions to be a sign of our disposition. For example, someone who refrains

ἀπεχόμενος τῶν σωματικῶν ἡδονῶν καὶ αὐτῷ
τούτῳ χαίρων σώφρων, ὁ δ' ἀχθόμενος ἀκόλαστος, καὶ ὁ μὲν ὑπομένων τὰ δεινὰ καὶ χαίρων ἢ
μὴ λυπούμενός γε ἀνδρεῖος, ὁ δὲ λυπούμενος δειλός. περὶ ἡδονὰς γὰρ καὶ λύπας ἐστὶν ἡ ἠθικὴ
ἀρετή· διὰ μὲν γὰρ τὴν ἡδονὴν τὰ φαῦλα πράττομεν, διὰ δὲ τὴν λύπην τῶν καλῶν ἀπεχόμεθα.
διὸ δεῖ ἦχθαί πως εὐθὺς ἐκ νέων, ὡς ὁ Πλάτων
φησίν, ὥστε χαίρειν τε καὶ λυπεῖσθαι οἷς δεῖ· . . .

[2.4] Ἀπορήσειε δ' ἄν τις πῶς λέγομεν ὅτι δεῖ τὰ
μὲν δίκαια πράττοντας δικαίους γίνεσθαι, τὰ δὲ

from bodily pleasures and is pleased at doing so has self-discipline, while someone who is displeased about refraining is self-indulgent. If you endure frightful things and are pleased by that—or at least not pained—you are brave, but you are a coward if it pains you. That is because virtue of character involves our feelings of pleasure and pain. We engage in bad acts because of pleasure and refrain from noble ones because of pain. That is why—as Plato says—we need to be raised in a particular way from childhood, so that we take pleasure in and are pained at the right things. . . .

After further remarks on pleasure, Aristotle opens chapter 4 with an argument that virtue is a matter not simply of doing the right thing, but of being firmly disposed to do it and having the right motivation.

[2.4] You might be puzzled about our claim that people must perform just acts in order to become just, and act with discipline in order to

σώφρονα σώφρονας· εἰ γὰρ πράττουσι τὰ δίκαια
καὶ σώφρονα, ἤδη εἰσὶ δίκαιοι καὶ σώφρονες,
ὥσπερ εἰ τὰ γραμματικὰ καὶ τὰ μουσικά, γραμμα-
τικοὶ καὶ μουσικοί. ἢ οὐδ' ἐπὶ τῶν τεχνῶν οὕτως
ἔχει; ἐνδέχεται γὰρ γραμματικόν τι ποιῆσαι καὶ
ἀπὸ τύχης καὶ ἄλλου ὑποθεμένου. τότε οὖν ἔσται
γραμματικός, ἐὰν καὶ γραμματικόν τι ποιήσῃ
καὶ γραμματικῶς· τοῦτο δ' ἐστὶ τὸ κατὰ τὴν ἐν
αὑτῷ γραμματικήν.

   ἔτι οὐδ' ὅμοιόν ἐστιν ἐπί τε τῶν τεχνῶν καὶ τῶν
ἀρετῶν· τὰ μὲν γὰρ ὑπὸ τῶν τεχνῶν γινόμενα τὸ
εὖ ἔχει ἐν αὑτοῖς· ἀρκεῖ οὖν ταῦτά πως ἔχοντα
γενέσθαι· τὰ δὲ κατὰ τὰς ἀρετὰς γινόμενα οὐκ ἐὰν
αὐτά πως ἔχῃ, δικαίως ἢ σωφρόνως πράττεται,
ἀλλὰ καὶ ἐὰν ὁ πράττων πῶς ἔχων πράττῃ,
πρῶτον μὲν ἐὰν εἰδώς, ἔπειτ' ἐὰν προαιρούμενος,

develop self-discipline. After all, if people perform just actions and acts of discipline, aren't they already just and self-disciplined—just as people who write are writers, and people who play music are musicians? But that isn't true even for those arts. You can write something correctly by chance, or at another's direction. You are a writer when you produce correct writing in a writerly way, making use of the art of writing inside yourself.

Also, there is a difference between virtues and arts. Whether the products of art are well made depends on their intrinsic features alone. It is enough that the products themselves possess certain features. But where the products of virtue are concerned, it is not *simply* by possessing certain features themselves that acts are performed justly or with self-discipline. The agents themselves must meet certain conditions when they perform them. They must act, first, with knowledge, second, on purpose (choosing the action for its own sake) and, third, they must

καὶ προαιρούμενος δι' αὐτά, τὸ δὲ τρίτον ἐὰν καὶ βεβαίως καὶ ἀμετακινήτως ἔχων πράττῃ. . . .

τὰ μὲν οὖν πράγματα δίκαια καὶ σώφρονα λέγεται, ὅταν ᾖ τοιαῦτα οἷα ἂν ὁ δίκαιος ἢ ὁ σώφρων πράξειεν· δίκαιος δὲ καὶ σώφρων ἐστὶν οὐχ ὁ ταῦτα πράττων, ἀλλὰ καὶ [ὁ] οὕτω πράττων ὡς οἱ δίκαιοι καὶ σώφρονες πράττουσιν. εὖ οὖν λέγεται ὅτι ἐκ τοῦ τὰ δίκαια πράττειν ὁ δίκαιος γίνεται καὶ ἐκ τοῦ τὰ σώφρονα ὁ σώφρων·

ἐκ δὲ τοῦ μὴ πράττειν ταῦτα οὐδεὶς ἂν οὐδὲ μελλήσειε γίνεσθαι ἀγαθός. ἀλλ' οἱ πολλοὶ ταῦτα μὲν οὐ πράττουσιν, ἐπὶ δὲ τὸν λόγον καταφεύγοντες οἴονται φιλοσοφεῖν καὶ οὕτως ἔσεσθαι σπουδαῖοι, ὅμοιόν τι ποιοῦντες τοῖς κάμνουσιν, οἳ

be firmly disposed to perform the action and unshakeable. . . .

Aristotle briefly explains why these three criteria don't apply in the case of arts, then returns to the case of virtue.
An act is called just or self-disciplined when it is the sort of thing a just person or a person with self-discipline would do. But a just or self-disciplined *person* isn't just someone who does these things; it is someone who does them in the way we mentioned, the way just or self-disciplined people act. It therefore makes perfect sense to say that a person becomes just from performing just acts and self-disciplined from acting with discipline.

There is no chance of becoming a good person if you don't perform those actions. Still, most people don't. They retreat to the comfort of theory, believing that they are practicing philosophy and that *it* will make them good people—like patients who listen carefully to the

τῶν ἰατρῶν ἀκούουσι μὲν ἐπιμελῶς, ποιοῦσι δ' οὐδὲν τῶν προσταττομένων. ὥσπερ οὖν οὐδ' ἐκεῖνοι εὖ ἕξουσι τὸ σῶμα οὕτω θεραπευόμενοι, οὐδ' οὗτοι τὴν ψυχὴν οὕτω φιλοσοφοῦντες.

[2.6] Δεῖ δὲ μὴ μόνον οὕτως εἰπεῖν, ὅτι ἕξις, ἀλλὰ καὶ ποία τις. ῥητέον οὖν ὅτι πᾶσα ἀρετή, οὗ ἂν ᾖ ἀρετή, αὐτό τε εὖ ἔχον ἀποτελεῖ καὶ τὸ ἔργον αὐτοῦ εὖ ἀποδίδωσιν, οἷον ἡ τοῦ ὀφθαλμοῦ ἀρετὴ τόν τε ὀφθαλμὸν σπουδαῖον ποιεῖ καὶ τὸ ἔργον αὐτοῦ· τῇ γὰρ τοῦ ὀφθαλμοῦ ἀρετῇ εὖ ὁρῶμεν. ὁμοίως ἡ τοῦ ἵππου ἀρετὴ ἵππον τε σπουδαῖον ποιεῖ καὶ ἀγαθὸν δραμεῖν καὶ ἐνεγκεῖν τὸν ἐπιβάτην καὶ μεῖναι τοὺς πολεμίους. εἰ δὴ τοῦτ' ἐπὶ πάντων οὕτως ἔχει, καὶ ἡ τοῦ ἀνθρώπου ἀρετὴ εἴη ἂν ἡ ἕξις ἀφ' ἧς ἀγαθὸς ἄνθρωπος γίνεται καὶ

doctors, but carry out none of their prescriptions. Well, that way of doing philosophy won't put their soul in good order, any more than that way of caring for their body will put it in good order.

In chapter 5 Aristotle explains that virtue is a disposition. In chapter 6 he specifies that it is a disposition that keeps us from going wrong in our feelings and actions.

[2.6] We should not simply state that virtue is a disposition; we should say what sort of disposition it is. Well, any virtue puts its possessor into good condition and makes it perform its activity well. The virtue of an eye, for example, makes the eye and its performance good; we see well because of the eye's virtue. Similarly, the virtue of a horse makes a horse good—good at running and carrying a rider and standing firm before the enemy. So, if the same principle holds in all cases, then for human beings as well, virtue would be a disposition by which we are good and by which

ἀφ' ἧς εὖ τὸ ἑαυτοῦ ἔργον ἀποδώσει. πῶς δὲ τοῦτ' ἔσται, ἤδη μὲν εἰρήκαμεν, ἔτι δὲ καὶ ὧδ' ἔσται φανερόν, ἐὰν θεωρήσωμεν ποία τίς ἐστιν ἡ φύσις αὐτῆς.

ἐν παντὶ δὴ συνεχεῖ καὶ διαιρετῷ ἔστι λαβεῖν τὸ μὲν πλεῖον τὸ δ' ἔλαττον τὸ δ' ἴσον, καὶ ταῦτα ἢ κατ' αὐτὸ τὸ πρᾶγμα ἢ πρὸς ἡμᾶς· τὸ δ' ἴσον μέσον τι ὑπερβολῆς καὶ ἐλλείψεως. λέγω δὲ τοῦ μὲν πράγματος μέσον τὸ ἴσον ἀπέχον ἀφ' ἑκατέρου τῶν ἄκρων, ὅπερ ἐστὶν ἓν καὶ τὸ αὐτὸ πᾶσιν, πρὸς ἡμᾶς δὲ ὃ μήτε πλεονάζει μήτε ἐλλείπει· τοῦτο δ' οὐχ ἕν, οὐδὲ ταὐτὸν πᾶσιν. οἷον εἰ τὰ δέκα πολλὰ τὰ δὲ δύο ὀλίγα, τὰ ἓξ μέσα λαμβάνουσι κατὰ τὸ πρᾶγμα· ἴσῳ γὰρ ὑπερέχει τε καὶ ὑπερέχεται· τοῦτο δὲ μέσον ἐστὶ κατὰ τὴν ἀριθμητικὴν ἀνα-λογίαν. τὸ δὲ πρὸς ἡμᾶς οὐχ οὕτω ληπτέον· οὐ

we perform our own activity well. We have already explained how that will happen, but we can also make it clear in the following way, if we think about the nature of a virtuous disposition.

MEANS AND EXTREMES

For anything that is continuous and divisible, it is possible to take more, or less, or an equal amount—either in terms of the thing itself, or in relation to us—and equality is a mean between excess and deficiency. By the mean *in the thing*, I mean what is equidistant from both extremes; it is one and the same for everyone. The mean *in relation to us*, on the other hand, is what isn't excessive or deficient, and that is not one and the same for everyone. For example, if ten is a lot and two is a little, then six is what you take in order to have the mean in the thing (since six exceeds and is exceeded by an equal amount; it is the arithmetical mean). But that is not how to take the mean relative to us. If ten

γὰρ εἴ τῳ δέκα μναῖ φαγεῖν πολὺ δύο δὲ ὀλίγον,
ὁ ἀλείπτης ἓξ μνᾶς προστάξει· ἔστι γὰρ ἴσως καὶ
τοῦτο πολὺ τῷ ληψομένῳ ἢ ὀλίγον· Μίλωνι μὲν
γὰρ ὀλίγον, τῷ δὲ ἀρχομένῳ τῶν γυμνασίων
πολύ. ὁμοίως ἐπὶ δρόμου καὶ πάλης. οὕτω δὴ πᾶς
ἐπιστήμων τὴν ὑπερβολὴν μὲν καὶ τὴν ἔλλειψιν
φεύγει, τὸ δὲ μέσον ζητεῖ καὶ τοῦθ᾽ αἱρεῖται, μέσον
δὲ οὐ τὸ τοῦ πράγματος ἀλλὰ τὸ πρὸς ἡμᾶς.

εἰ δὴ πᾶσα ἐπιστήμη οὕτω τὸ ἔργον εὖ ἐπιτε-
λεῖ, πρὸς τὸ μέσον βλέπουσα καὶ εἰς τοῦτο ἄγουσα
τὰ ἔργα. ... ἡ δ᾽ ἀρετὴ πάσης τέχνης ἀκριβεστέρα
καὶ ἀμείνων ἐστὶν ὥσπερ καὶ ἡ φύσις, τοῦ μέσου
ἂν εἴη στοχαστική. λέγω δὲ τὴν ἠθικήν· αὕτη γάρ
ἐστι περὶ πάθη καὶ πράξεις, ἐν δὲ τούτοις ἔστιν
ὑπερβολὴ καὶ ἔλλειψις καὶ τὸ μέσον. οἷον καὶ
φοβηθῆναι καὶ θαρρῆσαι καὶ ἐπιθυμῆσαι καὶ ὀργισθῆναι καὶ ἐλεῆσαι καὶ ὅλως ἡσθῆναι καὶ λυπη-
θῆναι ἔστι καὶ μᾶλλον καὶ ἧττον, καὶ ἀμφότερα
οὐκ εὖ· τὸ δ᾽ ὅτε δεῖ καὶ ἐφ᾽ οἷς καὶ πρὸς οὓς καὶ

minae of food is a lot to eat and two is not very much, an athletic trainer won't just tell you to eat six—because even that can be a lot for the recipient, or a little. (For Milo[9] it is only a little, but for a novice athlete it is a lot.) The same goes for running and wrestling. In fact, that's how any expert tries to avoid excess and deficiency, seeks out the mean, and selects it—not the mean of the thing, but the mean relative to us.

If that is how any expertise performs its activity well (by looking toward the mean and directing its activity toward it) . . . and if virtue, like nature, is better and more accurate than any art,[10] it follows that virtue is good at hitting the mean. I mean virtue of character, since it concerns feelings and actions, and these admit of excess, deficiency, and the mean. For example, we can feel fear and confidence, as well as appetite, anger, pity—indeed pleasure and displeasure quite generally—both too much and too little, and in neither case is it good. But to have such feelings at the right time, at the right

οὗ ἕνεκα καὶ ὡς δεῖ, μέσον τε καὶ ἄριστον, ὅπερ
ἐστὶ τῆς ἀρετῆς. ὁμοίως δὲ καὶ περὶ τὰς πράξεις
ἔστιν ὑπερβολὴ καὶ ἔλλειψις καὶ τὸ μέσον. ἡ δ᾽
ἀρετὴ περὶ πάθη καὶ πράξεις ἐστίν, ἐν οἷς ἡ μὲν
ὑπερβολὴ ἁμαρτάνεται καὶ ἡ ἔλλειψις [ψέγεται],
τὸ δὲ μέσον ἐπαινεῖται καὶ κατορθοῦται· ταῦτα δ᾽
ἄμφω τῆς ἀρετῆς. μεσότης τις ἄρα ἐστὶν ἡ ἀρετή,
στοχαστική γε οὖσα τοῦ μέσου. . . .

[2.7] . . . περὶ μὲν οὖν φόβους καὶ θάρρη ἀνδρεία μεσότης· τῶν δ᾽ ὑπερβαλλόντων ὁ μὲν τῇ

objects and people, with the right goal, and in the right manner, is intermediate and best; it is the mark of virtue. We can also be excessive, be deficient, or hit the mean *in our actions*, and virtue is about feelings *and* actions. When we go to excess or fall short we go wrong and are blamed, but hitting the mean is praised and keeps us on the correct path; both are marks of virtue. So virtue is an intermediate condition— insofar as it is good at hitting the mean. . . .

Over the rest of chapter 6 Aristotle notes that every virtue has two corresponding vices, one of excess and one of deficiency. In chapter 7 he applies this general account to give thumbnail sketches of particular virtues and vices.

Virtues and Vices

[2.7] . . . In matters of fear and daring, the intermediate condition is *bravery*. As for the excesses, there is no term for the overly fearless

ἀφοβίᾳ ἀνώνυμος (πολλὰ δ᾽ ἐστὶν ἀνώνυμα), ὁ δ᾽ ἐν τῷ θαρρεῖν ὑπερβάλλων θρασύς, ὁ δ᾽ ἐν τῷ μὲν φοβεῖσθαι ὑπερβάλλων τῷ δὲ θαρρεῖν ἐλλείπων δειλός.

περὶ ἡδονὰς δὲ καὶ λύπας—οὐ πάσας, ἧττον δὲ †καὶ† περὶ τὰς λύπας—μεσότης μὲν σωφροσύνη, ὑπερβολὴ δὲ ἀκολασία. ἐλλείποντες δὲ περὶ τὰς ἡδονὰς οὐ πάνυ γίνονται· διόπερ οὐδ᾽ ὀνόματος τετυχήκασιν οὐδ᾽ οἱ τοιοῦτοι, ἔστωσαν δὲ ἀναίσθητοι.

περὶ δὲ δόσιν χρημάτων καὶ λῆψιν μεσότης μὲν ἐλευθεριότης, ὑπερβολὴ δὲ καὶ ἔλλειψις ἀσωτία καὶ ἀνελευθερία. ἐναντίως δ᾽ ἐν αὐταῖς ὑπερβάλλουσι καὶ ἐλλείπουσιν· ὁ μὲν γὰρ ἄσωτος ἐν μὲν προέσει ὑπερβάλλει ἐν δὲ λήψει ἐλλείπει, ὁ δ᾽ ἀνελεύθερος ἐν μὲν λήψει ὑπερβάλλει ἐν δὲ προέσει ἐλλείπει. . . . περὶ δὲ χρήματα καὶ ἄλλαι διαθέσεις εἰσί, μεσότης μὲν μεγαλοπρέπεια (ὁ γὰρ μεγαλοπρεπὴς διαφέρει ἐλευθερίου· ὃ μὲν γὰρ περὶ μεγάλα, ὃ δὲ περὶ μικρά),

person (something we will see in other cases as well), but the overly daring person is *rash*. People who feel too much fear and too little daring are *cowards*.

In pleasures and pains—not all of them, and less so in the case of pain—the intermediate condition is *self-discipline*, and the excess is *self-indulgence*. It is rare for people to pursue pleasure too little, so we have no name for them. Let us call such people *impassive*.

Where giving away and taking in wealth is concerned, the intermediate condition is *generosity*, and the excess and deficiency are *extravagance* and *moneygrubbing*—which go to excess and fall sort in opposing ways. (The extravagant person gives away too much and takes in too little, while the *moneygrubber* goes to excess in taking and falls short in giving.) . . . In another set of attitudes toward wealth, the intermediate condition is *philanthropy*.[11] It differs from generosity in being about grand expenditures, while generosity is about giving on

ὑπερβολὴ δὲ ἀπειροκαλία καὶ βαναυσία, ἔλλειψις δὲ μικροπρέπεια· . . .

περὶ δὲ τιμὴν καὶ ἀτιμίαν μεσότης μὲν μεγαλοψυχία, ὑπερβολὴ δὲ χαυνότης τις λεγομένη, ἔλλειψις δὲ μικροψυχία· ὡς δ' ἐλέγομεν ἔχειν πρὸς τὴν μεγαλοπρέπειαν τὴν ἐλευθεριότητα, <τῷ> περὶ μικρὰ διαφέρουσαν, οὕτως ἔχει τις καὶ πρὸς τὴν μεγαλοψυχίαν, περὶ τιμὴν οὖσαν μεγάλην, αὐτὴ περὶ μικρὰν οὖσα· ἔστι γὰρ ὡς δεῖ ὀρέγεσθαι τιμῆς καὶ μᾶλλον ἢ δεῖ καὶ ἧττον, λέγεται δ' ὁ μὲν ὑπερβάλλων ταῖς ὀρέξεσι φιλότιμος, ὁ δ' ἐλλείπων ἀφιλότιμος, ὁ δὲ μέσος ἀνώνυμος. . . .

ἔστι δὲ καὶ περὶ τὴν ὀργὴν ὑπερβολὴ καὶ ἔλλειψις καὶ μεσότης, σχεδὸν δὲ ἀνωνύμων ὄντων αὐτῶν τὸν μέσον πρᾶον λέγοντες τὴν μεσότητα πραότητα καλέσωμεν· τῶν δ' ἄκρων ὁ μὲν

a smaller scale. Excess here is *tasteless vulgarity*, while deficiency is *shabbiness*. . . .

Where honor and dishonor are concerned, the intermediate condition is called *magnanimity*, and the excess is a kind of *conceit*, while the deficiency is *pusillanimity*. And there is another virtue that stands to magnanimity in the same relation that we said generosity stands to magnificence—that is, on a smaller scale. Magnanimity concerns great honors, while this virtue concerns smaller ones. It is possible to care about honor more than you should, less than you should, and in the right way. If you care too much, you are *status grubbing*, and if you care too little you are *unambitious*; there is no term for the person who strikes the mean. . . .

In anger too there is excess, deficiency, and the intermediate condition, none of which really has a name. Since we call people even tempered when they strike a middle course, let us call the intermediate condition *even temper*. As for the extremes, let us call the person who goes to

ὑπερβάλλων ὀργίλος ἔστω, ἡ δὲ κακία ὀργιλότης, ὁ δ' ἐλλείπων ἀόργητός τις, ἡ δ' ἔλλειψις
ἀοργησία.

εἰσὶ δὲ καὶ ἄλλαι τρεῖς μεσότητες, ἔχουσαι μέν
τινα ὁμοιότητα πρὸς ἀλλήλας, διαφέρουσαι δ' ἀλ-
λήλων· πᾶσαι μὲν γάρ εἰσι περὶ λόγων καὶ πράξεων κοινωνίαν, διαφέρουσι δὲ ὅτι ἣ μέν ἐστι περὶ
τἀληθὲς τὸ ἐν αὐτοῖς, αἳ δὲ περὶ τὸ ἡδύ· τούτου
δὲ τὸ μὲν ἐν παιδιᾷ τὸ δ' ἐν πᾶσι τοῖς κατὰ τὸν
βίον. . . . περὶ μὲν οὖν τὸ ἀληθὲς ὁ μὲν μέσος ἀλη-
θής τις καὶ ἡ μεσότης ἀλήθεια λεγέσθω, ἡ δὲ
προσποίησις ἡ μὲν ἐπὶ τὸ μεῖζον ἀλαζονεία καὶ ὁ
ἔχων αὐτὴν ἀλαζών, ἡ δ' ἐπὶ τὸ ἔλαττον εἰρωνεία
καὶ εἴρων <ὁ ἔχων>. περὶ δὲ τὸ ἡδὺ τὸ μὲν ἐν παιδιᾷ ὁ μὲν μέσος εὐτράπελος καὶ ἡ διάθεσις εὐτρα-
πελία, ἡ δ' ὑπερβολὴ βωμολοχία καὶ ὁ ἔχων αὐτὴν
βωμολόχος, ὁ δ' ἐλλείπων ἄγροικός τις καὶ ἡ ἕξις

excess *hot tempered*, and the vice *hot temper*. Someone deficient in anger is *meek*, so let us call that vice *meekness*.

Three other intermediate conditions are similar to each other but distinct. All of them concern what we say and do in social situations. One of them concerns telling the truth, while the others concern being pleasant (one of them in the context of telling jokes, the other in all contexts of life). . . . Where telling the truth is concerned, let us call the person who strikes the mean *honest* and the intermediate condition *honesty*. Pretending to be greater than you are is *bragging*, and someone who does that is a *braggart*, while pretending to be lesser is *dissembling* and whoever does that is a *dissembler*. As for being pleasant when telling jokes, the person who strikes the mean *has a good sense of humor*, and the condition is *a good sense of humor*. The excess is *buffoonery*, and someone who goes to excess is a *buffoon*. The deficient person is a *boor*, and the disposition is

ἀγροικία· περὶ δὲ τὸ λοιπὸν ἡδὺ τὸ ἐν τῷ βίῳ
ὁ μὲν ὡς δεῖ ἡδὺς ὢν φίλος καὶ ἡ μεσότης φιλία,
ὁ δ᾽ ὑπερβάλλων, εἰ μὲν οὐδενὸς ἕνεκα, ἄρεσκος,
εἰ δ᾽ ὠφελείας τῆς αὑτοῦ, κόλαξ, ὁ δ᾽ ἐλλείπων
καὶ ἐν πᾶσιν ἀηδὴς δύσερίς τις καὶ δύσκολος. . . .

[2.9] Ὅτι μὲν οὖν ἐστὶν ἡ ἀρετὴ ἡ ἠθικὴ μεσότης,
καὶ πῶς, καὶ ὅτι μεσότης δύο κακιῶν, τῆς μὲν καθ᾽
ὑπερβολὴν τῆς δὲ κατ᾽ ἔλλειψιν, καὶ ὅτι τοιαύτη
ἐστὶ διὰ τὸ στοχαστικὴ τοῦ μέσου εἶναι τοῦ ἐν τοῖς

boorishness. As for being pleasant in the rest of life, someone who does that appropriately is *friendly,* and the intermediate condition is *friendliness.* People who go to excess are *obsequious* if they have no ulterior motive; they are *panderers* if they do it to advance their own interest. People who fall short and are unpleasant in all situations are *contentious* and *disagreeable....*

In chapter 8 Aristotle makes some technical points about means and extremes. In chapter 9 he offers practical advice for people who seek to become virtuous.

ADVICE FOR BEGINNERS

[2.9] We have said enough to establish that virtue of character is an intermediate condition, and in what sense: that it is intermediate between two vices—one of excess and one of deficiency—and that it is intermediate by being

πάθεσι καὶ ἐν ταῖς πράξεσιν, ἱκανῶς εἴρηται. διὸ καὶ ἔργον ἐστὶ σπουδαῖον εἶναι. ἐν ἑκάστῳ γὰρ τὸ μέσον λαβεῖν ἔργον, οἷον κύκλου τὸ μέσον οὐ παντὸς ἀλλὰ τοῦ εἰδότος· οὕτω δὲ καὶ τὸ μὲν ὀργισθῆναι παντὸς καὶ ῥάδιον, καὶ τὸ δοῦναι ἀργύριον καὶ δαπανῆσαι· τὸ δ᾽ ᾧ καὶ ὅσον καὶ ὅτε καὶ οὗ ἕνεκα καὶ ὥς, οὐκέτι παντὸς οὐδὲ ῥάδιον· διόπερ τὸ εὖ καὶ σπάνιον καὶ ἐπαινετὸν καὶ καλόν.

διὸ δεῖ τὸν στοχαζόμενον τοῦ μέσου πρῶτον μὲν ἀποχωρεῖν τοῦ μᾶλλον ἐναντίου, καθάπερ καὶ ἡ Καλυψὼ παραινεῖ τούτου μὲν καπνοῦ καὶ κύματος ἐκτὸς ἔεργε νῆα. τῶν γὰρ ἄκρων τὸ μέν ἐστιν ἁμαρτωλότερον τὸ δ᾽ ἧττον· ἐπεὶ οὖν τοῦ μέσου τυχεῖν ἄκρως χαλεπόν, κατὰ τὸν δεύτερον, φασί, πλοῦν τὰ ἐλάχιστα ληπτέον τῶν κακῶν· τοῦτο δ᾽ ἔσται μάλιστα τοῦτον τὸν τρόπον ὃν λέγομεν. σκοπεῖν δὲ δεῖ πρὸς ἃ καὶ αὐτοὶ εὐκατάφοροί

good at hitting the mean in both feelings and actions. From this it follows that being good is hard work, since it is hard work to find the mean in a particular case. For example, not just anyone can find the middle of a circle; it takes someone who knows. In the same way, anyone can feel anger or give and spend money; that is easy. But it is not easy to do so to the right recipients, in the right amounts, at the right time, with the right goal, and in the right manner. Not everyone can do it. That is why doing well is rare, praiseworthy, and splendid.

It is also why someone trying to hit the mean should first of all pull away from the extreme that is more opposed. As Calypso advises, "steer your ship away from the surge and spray"[12]—because one of the two extremes is more gravely in error, the other less so. Since hitting upon the mean precisely is difficult, the next best course is to take the lesser evil. As for the best way to do that, here is our advice. You need to find out what you yourself are most susceptible to, since

ἐσμεν· ἄλλοι γὰρ πρὸς ἄλλα πεφύκαμεν· τοῦτο δ᾽ ἔσται γνώριμον ἐκ τῆς ἡδονῆς καὶ τῆς λύπης τῆς γινομένης περὶ ἡμᾶς. εἰς τοὐναντίον δ᾽ ἑαυτοὺς ἀφέλκειν δεῖ· πολὺ γὰρ ἀπάγοντες τοῦ ἁμαρτά- νειν εἰς τὸ μέσον ἥξομεν, ὅπερ οἱ τὰ διεστραμμένα τῶν ξύλων ὀρθοῦντες ποιοῦσιν. ἐν παντὶ δὲ μάλι- στα φυλακτέον τὸ ἡδὺ καὶ τὴν ἡδονήν· οὐ γὰρ ἀδέκαστοι κρίνομεν αὐτήν. ὅπερ οὖν οἱ δημο- γέροντες ἔπαθον πρὸς τὴν Ἑλένην, τοῦτο δεῖ πα- θεῖν καὶ ἡμᾶς πρὸς τὴν ἡδονήν, καὶ ἐν πᾶσι τὴν ἐκείνων ἐπιλέγειν φωνήν· οὕτω γὰρ αὐτὴν ἀπο- πεμπόμενοι ἧττον ἁμαρτησόμεθα. ταῦτ᾽ οὖν ποιοῦντες, ὡς ἐν κεφαλαίῳ εἰπεῖν, μάλιστα δυνη- σόμεθα τοῦ μέσου τυγχάνειν.

χαλεπὸν δ᾽ ἴσως τοῦτο, καὶ μάλιστ᾽ ἐν τοῖς καθ᾽ ἕκαστον· οὐ γὰρ ῥάδιον διορίσαι καὶ πῶς καὶ τίσι καὶ ἐπὶ ποίοις καὶ πόσον χρόνον ὀργιστέον· καὶ γὰρ ἡμεῖς ὁτὲ μὲν τοὺς ἐλλείποντας ἐπαινοῦμεν καὶ πράους φαμέν, ὁτὲ δὲ τοὺς χαλεπαίνοντας ἀνδρώδεις ἀποκαλοῦντες. ἀλλ᾽ ὁ μὲν μικρὸν τοῦ

people naturally differ on this (you can identify what it is for you from the pleasures and pains that you feel). And then you need to pull yourself away in the opposite direction, since by pulling hard against one fault, you get to the mean (as when straightening out warped planks). In every case, we must be especially on our guard against what we enjoy—that is, pleasure— since we are not impartial judges of it. We should react to pleasure the way the Trojan elders did toward Helen, and repeat their words.[13] If we dismiss pleasure like that in every case, we will go wrong less often. These, in short, are the strategies that will maximize our chances of hitting the mean.

It is of course still a difficult thing to do, especially in particular cases. It is not easy, for example, to determine how and at whom to get angry, for what sorts of offenses, and for how long. In fact, we sometimes praise people who fall short, calling them even tempered, or we call harsh people manly. In any case, we don't blame

εὖ παρεκβαίνων οὐ ψέγεται, οὔτ' ἐπὶ τὸ μᾶλλον οὔτ' ἐπὶ τὸ ἧττον, ὁ δὲ πλέον· οὗτος γὰρ οὐ λανθάνει. ὁ δὲ μέχρι τίνος καὶ ἐπὶ πόσον ψεκτὸς οὐ ῥάδιον τῷ λόγῳ ἀφορίσαι· οὐδὲ γὰρ ἄλλο οὐδὲν τῶν αἰσθητῶν· τὰ δὲ τοιαῦτα ἐν τοῖς καθ' ἕκαστα, καὶ ἐν τῇ αἰσθήσει ἡ κρίσις.

τὸ μὲν ἄρα τοσοῦτο δηλοῖ ὅτι ἡ μέση ἕξις ἐν πᾶσιν ἐπαινετή, ἀποκλίνειν δὲ δεῖ ὁτὲ μὲν ἐπὶ τὴν ὑπερβολὴν ὁτὲ δ' ἐπὶ τὴν ἔλλειψιν· οὕτω γὰρ ῥᾷστα τοῦ μέσου καὶ τοῦ εὖ τευξόμεθα.

people who miss the mean only slightly in either direction. It is someone who misses by a lot who gets blamed, because that is hard to miss. As for how long and how much they should be blamed, it is not easy to capture in a formula, since that isn't easy in any perceptual matter. It depends on the particular facts, where the judgment depends on perception.

We have said enough to establish that the intermediate disposition is praiseworthy in every case, but that in some cases we should lean toward the excess, and in others we should lean toward the deficiency. That is the easiest way for us to hit upon the mean and the good.

[3.1] Τῆς ἀρετῆς δὴ περὶ πάθη τε καὶ πράξεις οὔσης, καὶ ἐπὶ μὲν τοῖς ἑκουσίοις ἐπαίνων καὶ ψόγων γινομένων, ἐπὶ δὲ τοῖς ἀκουσίοις συγγνώμης, ἐνίοτε δὲ καὶ ἐλέου, τὸ ἑκούσιον καὶ τὸ ἀκούσιον ἀναγκαῖον ἴσως διορίσαι τοῖς περὶ ἀρετῆς ἐπισκοποῦσι, χρήσιμον δὲ καὶ τοῖς νομοθετοῦσι πρός τε τὰς τιμὰς καὶ τὰς κολάσεις.

3. TAKING RESPONSIBILITY

(Book 3)

The first five chapters of book 3 consider the role our actions and choices play in the expression and acquisition of virtue. The discussion culminates in an argument that we are responsible for our states of character and begins with an account of what makes our actions "voluntary" or "up to us."

[3.1] Now virtue involves both feelings *and* actions. What we do voluntarily gets praised and blamed, while we receive forgiveness (and sometimes even pity) for what we do involuntarily. So our inquiry into virtue presumably ought to demarcate what is voluntary and what is involuntary. The topic would also be useful for those formulating laws about rewards and punishments.

δοκεῖ δὴ ἀκούσια εἶναι τὰ βίᾳ ἢ δι' ἄγνοιαν γι-
νόμενα· βίαιον δὲ οὗ ἡ ἀρχὴ ἔξωθεν, τοιαύτη οὖσα
ἐν ᾗ μηδὲν συμβάλλεται ὁ πράττων ἢ ὁ πάσχων,
οἷον εἰ πνεῦμα κομίσαι ποι ἢ ἄνθρωποι κύριοι
ὄντες.

ὅσα δὲ διὰ φόβον μειζόνων κακῶν πράττεται
ἢ διὰ καλόν τι, οἷον εἰ τύραννος προστάττοι αἰσχρόν τι πρᾶξαι κύριος ὢν γονέων καὶ τέκνων, καὶ
πράξαντος μὲν σῴζοιντο μὴ πράξαντος δ' ἀπο-
θνήσκοιεν, ἀμφισβήτησιν ἔχει πότερον ἀκούσιά
ἐστιν ἢ ἑκούσια. τοιοῦτον δέ τι συμβαίνει καὶ περὶ
τὰς ἐν τοῖς χειμῶσιν ἐκβολάς· ἁπλῶς μὲν γὰρ οὐδεὶς ἀποβάλλεται ἑκών, ἐπὶ σωτηρίᾳ δ' αὐτοῦ
καὶ τῶν λοιπῶν ἅπαντες οἱ νοῦν ἔχοντες. μικταὶ
μὲν οὖν εἰσιν αἱ τοιαῦται πράξεις, ἐοίκασι δὲ μᾶλλον ἑκουσίοις· αἱρεταὶ γάρ εἰσι τότε ὅτε πράττο-
νται . . . καὶ γὰρ ἡ ἀρχὴ τοῦ κινεῖν τὰ ὀργανικὰ

Well, what seems involuntary is either forced or due to ignorance. What is forced has an external origin, which means that the agent, or rather patient, contributes nothing; for example, if you are carried off somewhere by strong winds, or by kidnappers.

When actions are done from fear of greater evils, or because of some noble cause—for example, if a tyrant who holds your parents and children hostage commands you to perform a shameful act, and your family will be saved if you do it but will die if you don't—it is controversial whether what you do is voluntary or involuntary. There is a similar dispute about captains who jettison the ship's cargo during a storm, since the act itself is something no one would do voluntarily, but anyone with sense would do it to save their own life and the lives of the other people on board. Well, such actions are mixed, although they are more like voluntary acts, since they are choice-worthy when they are performed. . . . Indeed,

μέρη ἐν ταῖς τοιαύταις πράξεσιν ἐν αὐτῷ ἐστίν· ὧν δ' ἐν αὐτῷ ἡ ἀρχή, ἐπ' αὐτῷ καὶ τὸ πράττειν καὶ μή. ἑκούσια δὴ τὰ τοιαῦτα, ἁπλῶς δ' ἴσως ἀκούσια· οὐδεὶς γὰρ ἂν ἕλοιτο καθ' αὑτὸ τῶν τοιούτων οὐδέν. . . .

εἰ δέ τις τὰ ἡδέα καὶ τὰ καλὰ φαίη βίαια εἶναι (ἀναγκάζειν γὰρ ἔξω ὄντα), πάντα ἂν εἴη αὐτῷ βίαια· τούτων γὰρ χάριν πάντες πάντα πράττου-σιν. καὶ οἱ μὲν βίᾳ καὶ ἄκοντες λυπηρῶς, οἱ δὲ διὰ τὸ ἡδὺ καὶ καλὸν μεθ' ἡδονῆς· γελοῖον δὲ τὸ αἰτιᾶσθαι τὰ ἐκτός, ἀλλὰ μὴ αὑτὸν εὐθήρατον ὄντα ὑπὸ τῶν τοιούτων, καὶ τῶν μὲν καλῶν ἑαυ-τόν, τῶν δ' αἰσχρῶν τὰ ἡδέα. ἔοικε δὴ τὸ βίαιον εἶναι οὗ ἔξωθεν ἡ ἀρχή, μηδὲν συμβαλλομένου τοῦ βιασθέντος. . . .

in such actions, the origin of the bodily movement is in the agent, and if the origin is in you, it is up to you whether you do the act or not. So such acts are voluntary, although perhaps in themselves they are involuntary, because no one would choose to do any such act for itself. . . .

If someone said that pleasant and noble opportunities force us to act (since they compel us from the outside) then *all* actions would be involuntary, as far as they are concerned. That's because the pleasant and the noble are everyone's reason for doing whatever they do. Besides, a forced and involuntary act is painful, while an act you do because it is pleasant or noble is performed with pleasure. It is ridiculous to blame the externals instead of yourself for being so susceptible to them — or to take responsibility for your noble acts but blame your shameful acts on the pleasant externals. So it does seem that what is forced has an external origin, with the forced person contributing nothing. . . .

ἀγνοεῖ μὲν οὖν πᾶς ὁ μοχθηρὸς ἃ δεῖ πράττειν καὶ
ὧν ἀφεκτέον, καὶ διὰ τὴν τοιαύτην ἁμαρτίαν ἄδικοι καὶ ὅλως κακοὶ γίνονται· τὸ δ’ ἀκούσιον
βούλεται λέγεσθαι οὐκ εἴ τις ἀγνοεῖ τὰ συμφέρο-
ντα· οὐ γὰρ ἡ ἐν τῇ προαιρέσει ἄγνοια αἰτία τοῦ
ἀκουσίου ἀλλὰ τῆς μοχθηρίας, οὐδ’ ἡ καθόλου
(ψέγονται γὰρ διά γε ταύτην) ἀλλ’ ἡ καθ’ ἕκαστα, ἐν οἷς καὶ περὶ ἃ ἡ πρᾶξις· ἐν τούτοις γὰρ καὶ
ἔλεος καὶ συγγνώμη· ὁ γὰρ τούτων τι ἀγνοῶν
ἀκουσίως πράττει. . . .

οἰηθείη δ’ ἄν τις καὶ τὸν υἱὸν πολέμιον εἶναι
ὥσπερ ἡ Μερόπη, καὶ ἐσφαιρῶσθαι τὸ λελογχω-
μένον δόρυ, ἢ τὸν λίθον κίσηριν εἶναι· καὶ ἐπὶ

Having concluded his discussion of forced action, Aristotle next turns to actions that are involuntary as a result of ignorance.

[3.1, *continued*] Now bad people are ignorant of what they should and shouldn't do, and this kind of error makes them unjust and vicious. However, we don't say people act involuntarily if they are ignorant of what would be good to do. That's because ignorance in what you choose makes you a bad person; it doesn't make your action involuntary. And we don't call someone's action involuntary if they are ignorant of the universal;[14] that is grounds for blame. Rather, it is ignorance of the particular facts about the action and its circumstances that makes an action involuntary. Whether you receive pity or forgiveness depends on the particular facts, and that is because you act involuntarily when you are ignorant of such things. . . .

For example, you might mistakenly think your son is the enemy, as Merope did,[15] or that a sharpened spear has a rounded tip, or that a

σωτηρίᾳ πίσας ἀποκτείναι ἄν· καὶ θῖξαι βουλόμε-
νος, ὥσπερ οἱ ἀκροχειριζόμενοι, πατάξειεν ἄν.
περὶ πάντα δὴ ταῦτα τῆς ἀγνοίας οὔσης, ἐν οἷς ἡ
πρᾶξις, ὁ τούτων τι ἀγνοήσας ἄκων δοκεῖ πεπρα-
χέναι, καὶ μάλιστα ἐν τοῖς κυριωτάτοις· . . .

 Ὄντος δ' ἀκουσίου τοῦ βίᾳ καὶ δι' ἄγνοιαν, τὸ
ἑκούσιον δόξειεν ἂν εἶναι οὗ ἡ ἀρχὴ ἐν αὐτῷ
εἰδότι τὰ καθ' ἕκαστα ἐν οἷς ἡ πρᾶξις. . . .

hard rock is only pumice. Or you might administer a potion in order to cure someone, but kill him instead. Or you might intend to grapple with your opponent, as wrestlers do, but deliver a blow instead. You can be ignorant of any of these facts about an action, and anyone who acts in such ignorance has acted involuntarily, especially if it is ignorance of the most important facts. . . .

Since involuntary action is either forced or due to ignorance, it would seem that a voluntary action is one whose origin is in the agent, and the agent knows the particular facts about the action. . . .

In the rest of chapter 1 Aristotle rejects the proposal that actions due to anger or appetite are involuntary. In chapters 2 through 4 he contrasts voluntariness, which belongs to all animals, with the distinctively human power of choosing our actions after due deliberation. Our character is revealed not simply by what we do, but by what

[3.5] . . . τὸ δὲ λέγειν ὡς οὐδεὶς ἑκὼν πονηρὸς
οὐδ' ἄκων μακάριος ἔοικε τὸ μὲν ψευδεῖ τὸ δ'
ἀληθεῖ· μακάριος μὲν γὰρ οὐδεὶς ἄκων, ἡ δὲ μοχθηρία ἑκούσιον. ἢ τοῖς γε νῦν εἰρημένοις ἀμφι-
σβητητέον, καὶ τὸν ἄνθρωπον οὐ φατέον ἀρχὴν
εἶναι οὐδὲ γεννητὴν τῶν πράξεων ὥσπερ καὶ τέκνων. εἰ δὲ ταῦτα φαίνεται καὶ μὴ ἔχομεν εἰς ἄλλας
ἀρχὰς ἀναγαγεῖν παρὰ τὰς ἐν ἡμῖν, ὧν καὶ αἱ ἀρχαὶ
ἐν ἡμῖν, καὶ αὐτὰ ἐφ' ἡμῖν καὶ ἑκούσια. τούτοις
δ' ἔοικε μαρτυρεῖσθαι καὶ ἰδίᾳ ὑφ' ἑκάστων καὶ
ὑπ' αὐτῶν τῶν νομοθετῶν· κολάζουσι γὰρ καὶ τι-
μωροῦνται τοὺς δρῶντας μοχθηρά, ὅσοι μὴ βίᾳ ἢ
δι' ἄγνοιαν ἧς μὴ αὐτοὶ αἴτιοι . . . καὶ γὰρ ἐπ'
αὐτῷ τῷ ἀγνοεῖν κολάζουσιν, ἐὰν αἴτιος εἶναι
δοκῇ τῆς ἀγνοίας, οἷον τοῖς μεθύουσι διπλᾶ τὰ
ἐπιτίμια· ἡ γὰρ ἀρχὴ ἐν αὐτῷ· κύριος γὰρ τοῦ μὴ

we do it for, he explains. In chapter 5 Aristotle argues for the voluntariness of character itself.

[3.5] . . . To say that no one is voluntarily bad — or involuntarily happy — seems partly false and partly true.[16] While no one is happy against their will, vice is in fact voluntary. Otherwise, we will have to dispute what we said above and deny that human beings originate and generate their actions as they do their children. But if all that seems right, and actions do originate in us without being drawn back to principles beyond ourselves, then those actions are up to us and voluntary. As a testament to this assumption, consider what both private citizens and legislators do: they punish or exact vengeance upon people who perform bad actions, as long as they are not forced or acting because of ignorance that is not their own fault. . . . Indeed, they even punish people for being ignorant, if it seems they are responsible for the ignorance. For example, the penalty is doubled when the perpetrators are drunk, because the ignorance

μεθυσθῆναι, τοῦτο δ᾽ αἴτιον τῆς ἀγνοίας. . . .
ὁμοίως δὲ καὶ ἐν τοῖς ἄλλοις, ὅσα δι᾽ ἀμέλειαν
ἀγνοεῖν δοκοῦσιν, ὡς ἐπ᾽ αὐτοῖς ὂν τὸ μὴ ἀγνο-
εῖν· τοῦ γὰρ ἐπιμεληθῆναι κύριοι.

ἀλλ᾽ ἴσως τοιοῦτός ἐστιν ὥστε μὴ ἐπιμεληθῆναι. ἀλλὰ τοῦ τοιούτους γενέσθαι αὐτοὶ αἴτιοι ζῶν-
τες ἀνειμένως, καὶ τοῦ ἀδίκους ἢ ἀκολάστους
εἶναι, οἳ μὲν κακουργοῦντες, οἳ δὲ ἐν πότοις καὶ
τοῖς τοιούτοις διάγοντες· αἱ γὰρ περὶ ἕκαστα ἐνέργειαι τοιούτους ποιοῦσιν. τοῦτο δὲ δῆλον ἐκ τῶν
μελετώντων πρὸς ἡντινοῦν ἀγωνίαν ἢ πρᾶξιν· δια-
τελοῦσι γὰρ ἐνεργοῦντες. τὸ μὲν οὖν ἀγνοεῖν ὅτι
ἐκ τοῦ ἐνεργεῖν περὶ ἕκαστα αἱ ἕξεις γίνονται,
κομιδῇ ἀναισθήτου. . . .

εἰ δὲ μὴ ἀγνοῶν τις πράττει ἐξ ὧν ἔσται ἄδικος, ἑκὼν ἄδικος ἂν εἴη, οὐ μὴν ἐάν γε βούληται,

originates in them. They were in control of not getting drunk, and that was the cause of their ignorance. . . . So too in other cases where it seems people are ignorant as a result of carelessness. The assumption is that it was up to them not to be ignorant, since it was in their power to take care.

But perhaps they are the sort of person who does not take care? Still, they are responsible for having become that sort of person, by living without restraint—and for becoming unjust by acting badly, or for becoming self-indulgent by spending their time in drinking and the like; the activities in each case make you that sort of person. This is clear in the case of athletes who are training for a particular contest or event, who continually perform the activity. Anyone with any sense will know that we develop our disposition in a particular domain from what we do in that domain. . . .

People who knowingly do what will make themselves unjust are voluntarily unjust.

ἄδικος ὢν παύσεται καὶ ἔσται δίκαιος. οὐδὲ γὰρ
ὁ νοσῶν ὑγιής. καὶ εἰ οὕτως ἔτυχεν, ἑκὼν νοσεῖ,
ἀκρατῶς βιοτεύων καὶ ἀπειθῶν τοῖς ἰατροῖς. τότε
μὲν οὖν ἐξῆν αὐτῷ μὴ νοσεῖν, προεμένῳ δ' οὐκέτι,
ὥσπερ οὐδ' ἀφέντι λίθον ἔτ' αὐτὸν δυνατὸν ἀνα-
λαβεῖν· ἀλλ' ὅμως ἐπ' αὐτῷ τὸ βαλεῖν [καὶ
ῥῖψαι]· ἡ γὰρ ἀρχὴ ἐν αὐτῷ. οὕτω δὲ καὶ τῷ ἀδίκῳ
καὶ τῷ ἀκολάστῳ ἐξ ἀρχῆς μὲν ἐξῆν τοιούτοις μὴ
γενέσθαι, διὸ ἑκόντες εἰσίν· γενομένοις δ' οὐκέτι
ἔστι μὴ εἶναι. . . .

εἰ δέ τις λέγοι ὅτι πάντες ἐφίενται τοῦ φαινο-
μένου ἀγαθοῦ, τῆς δὲ φαντασίας οὐ κύριοι, ἀλλ'
ὁποῖός ποθ' ἕκαστός ἐστι, τοιοῦτο καὶ τὸ τέλος

Nonetheless, this does not mean that a person will stop being unjust, and will be a just person, simply by wanting to be so. An invalid will not become healthy just by wanting to, either. Still, their illness is voluntary if they became ill by living a dissolute life and disregarding medical advice. It was up to them, earlier, not to be ill, but once they have let themselves go, that is no longer the case—just as it is no longer possible for you to take back a stone you have thrown away—but nonetheless, throwing it away was up to you, since the origin was in you. In the same way, it was possible in the beginning for the unjust or self-indulgent person not to become that kind of person, which is why they are like that voluntarily. But having become that sort of person, it is no longer possible for them not to be like that. . . .

Suppose someone objects that we all pursue what appears *to us* to be good, but are not in control of the appearance—that the sort of person you are determines how the goal appears

φαίνεται αὐτῷ· εἰ μὲν οὖν ἕκαστος ἑαυτῷ τῆς
ἕξεώς ἐστί πως αἴτιος, καὶ τῆς φαντασίας ἔσται
πως αὐτὸς αἴτιος· . . .

εἰ οὖν, ὥσπερ λέγεται, ἑκούσιοί εἰσιν αἱ ἀρεταί
(καὶ γὰρ τῶν ἕξεων συναίτιοί πως αὐτοί ἐσμεν, καὶ
τῷ ποιοί τινες εἶναι τὸ τέλος τοιόνδε τιθέμεθα),
καὶ αἱ κακίαι ἑκούσιοι ἂν εἶεν· ὁμοίως γάρ.

Κοινῇ μὲν οὖν περὶ τῶν ἀρετῶν εἴρηται ἡμῖν
τό τε γένος τύπῳ, ὅτι μεσότητές εἰσιν καὶ ὅτι
ἕξεις, ὑφ᾽ ὧν τε γίνονται, ὅτι τούτων πρακτι-
καὶ <καὶ> καθ᾽ αὑτάς, καὶ ὅτι ἐφ᾽ ἡμῖν καὶ ἑκούσιοι, καὶ οὕτως ὡς ἂν ὁ ὀρθὸς λόγος προστάξῃ.
οὐχ ὁμοίως δὲ αἱ πράξεις ἑκούσιοί εἰσι καὶ αἱ ἕξεις·
τῶν μὲν γὰρ πράξεων ἀπ᾽ ἀρχῆς μέχρι τοῦ τέλους
κύριοί ἐσμεν, εἰδότες τὰ καθ᾽ ἕκαστα, τῶν ἕξεων
δὲ τῆς ἀρχῆς, καθ᾽ ἕκαστα δὲ ἡ πρόσθεσις οὐ

to you. Well, if we are responsible in a way for forming our dispositions, we *are* responsible in a way for how the good appears to us. . . .

And if *the virtues* are voluntary, as people say they are (since we are in a way jointly responsible for our dispositions, and pursue the goals we do because of the type of person we are) then *the vices* would be voluntary as well, for the same reasons.

Well then, we have discussed the virtues in general and sketched their genus. They are intermediate conditions and dispositions. They dispose us to perform, for their own sakes, the sort of actions from which they arise. They are up to us and voluntary, and they operate as correct thinking would dictate. But actions and dispositions are not voluntary in the same way, for we are in control of voluntary actions from beginning to end, since we know the particulars. With dispositions, however, we are in control in the beginning, but the particular progression is

γνώριμος, ὥσπερ ἐπὶ τῶν ἀρρωστιῶν· ἀλλ᾽ ὅτι ἐφ᾽ ἡμῖν ἦν οὕτως ἢ μὴ οὕτω χρήσασθαι, διὰ τοῦτο ἑκούσιοι.

not obvious (as with failing health). Still, it *was* up to us whether or not we behaved in this way, and for that reason the dispositions are voluntary.

These chapters on voluntariness and related topics conclude Aristotle's general remarks about virtue of character.

Ἀναλαβόντες δὲ περὶ ἑκάστης εἴπωμεν τίνες εἰσὶ καὶ περὶ ποῖα καὶ πῶς· . . . καὶ πρῶτον περὶ ἀνδρείας.

[3.6] Ὅτι μὲν οὖν μεσότης ἐστὶ περὶ φόβους καὶ θάρρη, ἤδη φανερὸν γεγένηται· φοβούμεθα

4. VIRTUE AND VICE IN ACTION

(Books 3, 4, and 5)
Aristotle now embarks on a discussion of particular virtues and vices of character, which will occupy his attention through the end of book 5. In each case he identifies the mean and the extremes, and in keeping with his practical advice at the end of book 2, he often identifies the extreme that is "more opposed" to the mean, so that we can start out by seeking to avoid it.

MATTERS OF LIFE AND DEATH

Let us now take up the virtues individually and identify each by its objects and its orientation toward them. . . . First let us discuss bravery.

[3.6] By now it is clear that bravery is an intermediate disposition in matters of fear and

δὲ δῆλον ὅτι τὰ φοβερά, ταῦτα δ᾽ ἐστὶν ὡς ἁπλῶς εἰπεῖν κακά· διὸ καὶ τὸν φόβον ὁρίζονται προσδοκίαν κακοῦ. φοβούμεθα μὲν οὖν πάντα τὰ κακά, οἷον ἀδοξίαν πενίαν νόσον ἀφιλίαν θάνατον, ἀλλ᾽ οὐ περὶ πάντα δοκεῖ ὁ ἀνδρεῖος εἶναι· ἔνια γὰρ καὶ δεῖ φοβεῖσθαι καὶ καλόν, τὸ δὲ μὴ αἰσχρόν, οἷον ἀδοξίαν· ὁ μὲν γὰρ φοβούμενος ἐπιεικὴς καὶ αἰδήμων, ὁ δὲ μὴ φοβούμενος ἀναίσχυντος. . . . πενίαν δ᾽ ἴσως οὐ δεῖ φοβεῖσθαι οὐδὲ νόσον, οὐδ᾽ ὅλως ὅσα μὴ ἀπὸ κακίας μηδὲ δι᾽ αὐτόν. ἀλλ᾽ οὐδ᾽ ὁ περὶ ταῦτα ἄφοβος ἀνδρεῖος. . . . ἔνιοι γὰρ ἐν τοῖς πολεμικοῖς κινδύνοις δειλοὶ ὄντες ἐλευθέριοί εἰσι καὶ πρὸς χρημάτων ἀποβολὴν εὐθαρσῶς ἔχουσιν. οὐδὲ δὴ εἴ τις ὕβριν περὶ παῖδας καὶ γυναῖκα φοβεῖται . . . δειλός ἐστιν· οὐδ᾽ εἰ θαρρεῖ μέλλων μαστιγοῦσθαι, ἀνδρεῖος.

περὶ ποῖα οὖν τῶν φοβερῶν ὁ ἀνδρεῖος; ἢ περὶ τὰ μέγιστα; οὔθεὶς γὰρ ὑπομενετικώτερος τῶν

boldness. What we fear, evidently, are frightening things, and such things are, in a word, bad. That is why people define fear as expectation of something bad. But while all bad things are objects of fear—disrepute, poverty, disease, loneliness, death—we are not *brave* about all of them. That's because there are some things we should fear, and it is decent to fear them—for example, disgrace. You are decent and modest for fearing disgrace, and shameless if you don't. . . . Perhaps we should not be afraid of poverty or disease, or in general what is not due to vice or self-inflicted. But fearlessness about these is not bravery either. . . . People who are cowards on the battlefield may give freely to their friends and be quite bold about throwing away their money. And you are not a coward for being afraid that your child or wife will be assaulted . . . or brave if you are emboldened at the prospect of being whipped.

So which frightening things are the domain of bravery? Presumably the greatest ones, since

δεινῶν. φοβερώτατον δ᾽ ὁ θάνατος· ... δόξειε δ᾽ ἂν οὐδὲ περὶ θάνατον τὸν ἐν παντὶ ὁ ἀνδρεῖος εἶναι, οἷον ἐν θαλάττῃ ἢ νόσοις. ἐν τίσιν οὖν; ἢ ἐν τοῖς καλλίστοις; τοιοῦτοι δὲ οἱ ἐν πολέμῳ· ἐν μεγίστῳ γὰρ καὶ καλλίστῳ κινδύνῳ. ... κυρίως δὴ λέγοιτ᾽ ἂν ἀνδρεῖος ὁ περὶ τὸν καλὸν θάνατον ἀδεής, καὶ ὅσα θάνατον ἐπιφέρει ὑπόγυια ὄντα· τοιαῦτα δὲ μάλιστα τὰ κατὰ πόλεμον. οὐ μὴν ἀλλὰ καὶ ἐν θαλάττῃ καὶ ἐν νόσοις ἀδεὴς ὁ ἀνδρεῖος, οὐχ οὕτω δὲ ὡς οἱ θαλάττιοι· οἳ μὲν γὰρ ἀπεγνώκασι τὴν σωτηρίαν καὶ τὸν θάνατον τὸν τοιοῦτον δυσχεραίνουσιν, οἳ δὲ εὐέλπιδές εἰσι παρὰ τὴν ἐμπειρίαν. ἅμα δὲ καὶ ἀνδρίζονται ἐν οἷς ἐστὶν ἀλκὴ ἢ καλὸν τὸ ἀποθανεῖν· ἐν ταῖς τοιαύταις δὲ φθοραῖς οὐδέτερον ὑπάρχει.

no one endures more than the brave. The most frightening thing of all is death, . . . But not death in every situation, it seems, for example not at sea or from illness. So in which situations? Presumably in the noblest. Death in battle is of this sort, for the danger you face is both greatest and noblest. . . . You are properly called brave for being unafraid to die a noble death when the risk of death is right at hand; being in combat is especially like that. Nonetheless, a brave person *will* be fearless at sea and in illness, although not like seafarers who have given up all hope of safety (and bemoan a death of this sort) or are confident of their safety as a result of experience. Brave action occurs in situations where you can fight back, or it would be noble to die, neither of which is the case for death at sea or from illness.

"Noble" above is a translation for KALON, *which is Aristotle's term denoting the goodness specific to virtuous actions; it overlaps in different*

[3.7] Τὸ δὲ φοβερὸν οὐ πᾶσι μὲν τὸ αὐτό, λέγομεν δέ τι καὶ ὑπὲρ ἄνθρωπον. τοῦτο μὲν οὖν παντὶ
φοβερὸν τῷ γε νοῦν ἔχοντι· τὰ δὲ κατ' ἄνθρωπον διαφέρει μεγέθει καὶ τῷ μᾶλλον καὶ ἧττον·
ὁμοίως δὲ καὶ τὰ θαρραλέα. ὁ δὲ ἀνδρεῖος ἀνέκ-
πληκτος ὡς ἄνθρωπος. φοβήσεται μὲν οὖν καὶ τὰ
τοιαῦτα, ὡς δεῖ δὲ καὶ ὡς ὁ λόγος ὑπομενεῖ τοῦ
καλοῦ ἕνεκα· τοῦτο γὰρ τέλος τῆς ἀρετῆς.

ἔστι δὲ μᾶλλον καὶ ἧττον ταῦτα φοβεῖσθαι, καὶ
ἔτι τὰ μὴ φοβερὰ ὡς τοιαῦτα φοβεῖσθαι. . . . ὁ μὲν

*registers with "splendid," "noble," "honorable,"
"decent," "ethical," "fine," and even "beautiful." In the context of bravery, "noble" is a
good translation—given the enormous risk involved in the actions Aristotle counts as brave.
In the context of other virtues, "decent" is often
a better fit. The translation varies accordingly.*

[3.7] While not everyone is frightened by the
same things, we hold that some things are too
much for a human, and will frighten anyone
with sense. Other things are more and less
frightening to different people, and the same
goes for things that embolden us; bravery is a
matter of being as undaunted as a human can be.
Brave people *will* be frightened by such things,
but in the right way, and they will endure them
as thinking dictates. Their aim is to do what is
noble, since that is the goal of virtue.

It is possible to be more and less frightened
by frightening things, and also to be frightened
by things that are not frightening, as if they
were. . . . People who endure and are frightened

οὖν ἃ δεῖ καὶ οὗ ἕνεκα ὑπομένων καὶ φοβούμενος, καὶ ὡς δεῖ καὶ ὅτε, ὁμοίως δὲ καὶ θαρρῶν, ἀνδρεῖος· κατ' ἀξίαν γάρ, καὶ ὡς ἂν ὁ λόγος, πάσχει καὶ πράττει ὁ ἀνδρεῖος. . . .

τῶν δ' ὑπερβαλλόντων ὁ μὲν τῇ ἀφοβίᾳ ἀνώνυμος (εἴρηται δ' ἡμῖν ἐν τοῖς πρότερον ὅτι πολλά ἐστιν ἀνώνυμα), εἴη δ' ἄν τις μαινόμενος ἢ ἀνάλγητος, εἰ μηδὲν φοβοῖτο, μήτε σεισμὸν μήτε κύματα, καθάπερ φασὶ τοὺς Κελτούς· ὁ δὲ τῷ θαρρεῖν ὑπερβάλλων περὶ τὰ φοβερὰ θρασύς. δοκεῖ δὲ καὶ ἀλαζὼν εἶναι ὁ θρασὺς καὶ προσποιητικὸς ἀνδρείας· ὡς γοῦν ἐκεῖνος περὶ τὰ φοβερὰ ἔχει, οὗτος βούλεται φαίνεσθαι· ἐν οἷς οὖν δύναται, μιμεῖται. διὸ καὶ εἰσὶν οἱ πολλοὶ αὐτῶν θρασύδειλοι· ἐν τούτοις γὰρ θρασυνόμενοι τὰ φοβερὰ οὐχ ὑπομένουσιν. ὁ δὲ τῷ φοβεῖσθαι ὑπερβάλλων δειλός· καὶ γὰρ ἃ μὴ δεῖ καὶ ὡς οὐ δεῖ, καὶ πάντα

by the right things and for the right reasons, as well as in the right manner and at the right times—and likewise for what emboldens them—those people are brave. A brave person's suffering and action is worthwhile; it is what thinking would command. . . .

As for the extremes, there is no name for the overly fearless person. (As we mentioned above, many of these characters are nameless.) But you would be mad or incapable of feeling if you were frightened at nothing, not even at earthquakes or raging waves, as people say about the Celts. Someone who is excessively emboldened in the face of frightening things is rash—and seems to be a braggart as well, pretending to be brave. They want it to look as if they face frightening things the way the brave do, and so they imitate them as far as they can (which in fact makes most of them rash cowards, since they fail to withstand the frightening things that their boldness leads them to face). The excessively frightened person is a coward: frightened by the

τὰ τοιαῦτα ἀκολουθεῖ αὐτῷ. ἐλλείπει δὲ καὶ τῷ θαρρεῖν· ἀλλ᾽ ἐν ταῖς λύπαις ὑπερβάλλων μᾶλλον καταφανής ἐστιν. δύσελπις δή τις ὁ δειλός· πάντα γὰρ φοβεῖται. ὁ δ᾽ ἀνδρεῖος ἐναντίως· τὸ γὰρ θαρρεῖν εὐέλπιδος.

περὶ ταὐτὰ μὲν οὖν ἐστιν ὅ τε δειλὸς καὶ ὁ θρασὺς καὶ ὁ ἀνδρεῖος, διαφόρως δ᾽ ἔχουσι πρὸς αὐτά· οἱ μὲν γὰρ ὑπερβάλλουσι καὶ ἐλλείπουσιν, ὃ δὲ μέσως ἔχει καὶ ὡς δεῖ . . . καὶ ὅτι καλὸν αἱρεῖται καὶ ὑπομένει, ἢ ὅτι αἰσχρὸν τὸ μή. τὸ δ᾽ ἀποθνήσκειν φεύγοντα πενίαν ἢ ἔρωτα ἤ τι λυπηρὸν οὐκ ἀνδρείου, ἀλλὰ μᾶλλον δειλοῦ· μαλακία γὰρ τὸ φεύγειν τὰ ἐπίπονα, καὶ οὐχ ὅτι καλὸν ὑπομένει, ἀλλὰ φεύγων κακόν.

[3.8] Ἔστι μὲν οὖν ἡ ἀνδρεία τοιοῦτόν τι, λέγονται δὲ καὶ ἕτεραι κατὰ πέντε τρόπους· πρῶτον μὲν ἡ πολιτική· μάλιστα γὰρ ἔοικεν. δοκοῦσι γὰρ

wrong things or in the wrong way, and so forth. They also fall short in boldness, but they are more conspicuous in having excessive pains. A coward lacks confidence and is frightened by everything. A brave person is the opposite, because being bold makes you confident.

People are cowardly or rash or brave in relation to the same kinds of challenge; the difference is in how they are disposed to respond. The cowardly and the rash go too far and not far enough, while the brave strike a middle course and do as they should. . . . They make their decision and endure because it is noble to do so, or shameful not to. Dying to escape from poverty, erotic passion, or something painful is a mark not of bravery but of cowardice. That's because it is softness to flee from painful difficulty — to flee something bad — rather than to bear the burden because it is noble to do so.

[3.8] While bravery is the sort of thing we have described, people also speak of other forms of bravery, which fall into five types. The

ὑπομένειν τοὺς κινδύνους οἱ πολῖται διὰ τὰ ἐκ τῶν νόμων ἐπιτίμια καὶ τὰ ὀνείδη καὶ διὰ τὰς τιμάς· καὶ διὰ τοῦτο ἀνδρειότατοι δοκοῦσιν εἶναι παρ᾽ οἷς οἱ δειλοὶ ἄτιμοι καὶ οἱ ἀνδρεῖοι ἔντιμοι. . . . ὡμοίωται δ᾽ αὕτη μάλιστα τῇ πρότερον εἰρημένῃ, ὅτι δι᾽ ἀρετὴν γίνεται· δι᾽ αἰδῶ γὰρ καὶ διὰ καλοῦ ὄρεξιν (τιμῆς γάρ) καὶ φυγὴν ὀνείδους, αἰσχροῦ ὄντος.

τάξαι δ᾽ ἄν τις καὶ τοὺς ὑπὸ τῶν ἀρχόντων ἀναγκαζομένους εἰς ταὐτό· χείρους δ᾽, ὅσῳ οὐ δι᾽ αἰδῶ ἀλλὰ διὰ φόβον αὐτὸ δρῶσι, καὶ φεύγοντες οὐ τὸ αἰσχρὸν ἀλλὰ τὸ λυπηρόν· ἀναγκάζουσι γὰρ . . . οἱ προστάττοντες, κἂν ἀναχωρῶσι τύπτοντες, . . . καὶ οἱ πρὸ τῶν τάφρων καὶ τῶν τοιούτων παρατάττοντες· πάντες γὰρ

primary type is that of citizens, since it is most like bravery. It seems citizen soldiers submit to dangers because of legal penalties and reproaches and because they are rewarded with honor. That is why citizens appear to be bravest in cities where the cowardly are punished and the brave are rewarded. . . . This sort of bravery is most similar to the one we discussed above, insofar as it comes from virtue. That's because it is due to a sense of shame, a desire for honor (a noble thing), and an aversion to reproach (a shameful thing).

You might also classify as brave soldiers whose officers coerce them into facing dangers. But they are inferior insofar as they do not act from a sense of shame; they act from fear. What they seek to avoid is not disgrace but pain. Commanders coerce their troops . . . when, for example, they deliver a beating to anyone who retreats from their post, or when they station troops in front of a ditch or something like that. These are all cases of coercion. You should be

ἀναγκάζουσιν. δεῖ δ' οὐ δι' ἀνάγκην ἀνδρεῖον
εἶναι, ἀλλ' ὅτι καλόν.

δοκεῖ δὲ καὶ ἡ ἐμπειρία ἡ περὶ ἕκαστα ἀνδρεία
εἶναι· . . . ἐν τοῖς πολεμικοῖς δ' οἱ στρατιῶται·
δοκεῖ γὰρ εἶναι πολλὰ κενὰ τοῦ πολέμου, ἃ μάλιστα συνεωράκασιν οὗτοι· φαίνονται δὴ ἀνδρεῖοι,
ὅτι οὐκ ἴσασιν οἱ ἄλλοι οἷά ἐστιν. εἶτα ποιῆσαι καὶ
μὴ παθεῖν μάλιστα δύνανται ἐκ τῆς ἐμπειρίας, δυ-
νάμενοι χρῆσθαι τοῖς ὅπλοις καὶ τοιαῦτα ἔχοντες
ὁποῖα ἂν εἴη καὶ πρὸς τὸ ποιῆσαι καὶ πρὸς τὸ μὴ
παθεῖν κράτιστα· ὥσπερ οὖν ἀνόπλοις ὡπλισμέ-
νοι μάχονται καὶ ἀθληταὶ ἰδιώταις· . . .

οἱ στρατιῶται δὲ δειλοὶ γίνονται, ὅταν ὑπερ-
τείνῃ ὁ κίνδυνος καὶ λείπωνται τοῖς πλήθεσι καὶ
ταῖς παρασκευαῖς· πρῶτοι γὰρ φεύγουσι, τὰ δὲ
πολιτικὰ μένοντα ἀποθνήσκει . . . τοῖς μὲν γὰρ αἰσχρὸν τὸ φεύγειν καὶ ὁ θάνατος τῆς τοιαύτης

brave, however, because it is noble, not because you have been coerced into it.

Being experienced in a particular kind of danger also seems to be bravery, . . . and on the battlefield it is mercenaries who are experienced. There are many empty alarms in a battle, it seems, and these soldiers are best at recognizing them. So they appear brave when others don't know whether the alarm is real. Also, their experience makes them particularly good at doing their jobs without getting hurt, since they are adept at using their equipment, and have the kind that is best for getting the job done without being injured. So they fight like armed men against the unarmed, or athletes against ordinary people. . . .

Mercenaries turn into cowards when the danger is extreme, and they abandon their companies and their equipment. They are the first to flee, while citizen soldiers stand their ground and die. . . . The citizens stand their ground because they think fleeing is shameful;

σωτηρίας αἱρετώτερος· οἳ δὲ καὶ ἐξ ἀρχῆς ἐκινδύ-
νευον ὡς κρείττους ὄντες, γνόντες δὲ φεύγουσι,
τὸν θάνατον μᾶλλον τοῦ αἰσχροῦ φοβούμενοι· ὁ
δ᾽ ἀνδρεῖος οὐ τοιοῦτος.

καὶ τὸν θυμὸν δ᾽ ἐπὶ τὴν ἀνδρείαν φέρουσιν·
ἀνδρεῖοι γὰρ εἶναι δοκοῦσι καὶ οἱ διὰ θυμὸν ὥσπερ
τὰ θηρία ἐπὶ τοὺς τρώσαντας φερόμενα, ὅτι καὶ
οἱ ἀνδρεῖοι θυμοειδεῖς· ἰτητικώτατον γὰρ ὁ θυμὸς
πρὸς τοὺς κινδύνους. . . . οἱ μὲν οὖν ἀνδρεῖοι διὰ
τὸ καλὸν πράττουσιν, ὁ δὲ θυμὸς συνεργεῖ αὐτοῖς·
τὰ θηρία δὲ διὰ λύπην· διὰ γὰρ τὸ πληγῆναι ἢ διὰ
τὸ φοβεῖσθαι . . . οὐ δή ἐστιν ἀνδρεῖα διὰ τὸ ὑπ᾽
ἀλγηδόνος καὶ θυμοῦ ἐξελαυνόμενα πρὸς τὸν κίν-
δυνον ὁρμᾶν, οὐθὲν τῶν δεινῶν προορῶντα,
ἐπεὶ οὕτω γε κἂν οἱ ὄνοι ἀνδρεῖοι εἶεν πεινῶντες·
τυπτόμενοι γὰρ οὐκ ἀφίστανται τῆς νομῆς· . . .
φυσικωτάτη δ᾽ ἔοικεν ἡ διὰ τὸν θυμὸν εἶναι, καὶ

they prefer death to staying alive on those terms. Mercenaries, on the other hand, risk dangers at first when they think they hold the advantage but flee when they realize they do not; they fear death more than dishonor. That is not what a brave person is like.

Ferocity also gets confused with bravery. When people fight because they are enraged, like wounded animals launched at their attackers, they too appear brave, since a brave person does have a ferocious spirit; nothing is readier to meet dangers than spirit. . . . But brave people do what they do because it is noble, with their ferocious spirit helping them do it. Those animals, by contrast, act from pain; they attack because they have been struck or are afraid. . . . There is no bravery in rushing toward danger because you are driven by pains or by rage, with no thought of the perils ahead. Otherwise hungry donkeys would be brave, since even a beating won't stop them from grazing. . . . The bravery that is due to rage seems to be the most

προσλαβοῦσα προαίρεσιν καὶ τὸ οὗ ἕνεκα ἀνδρεία εἶναι. καὶ οἱ ἄνθρωποι δὴ ὀργιζόμενοι μὲν ἀλγοῦσι, τιμωρούμενοι δ᾽ ἥδονται· οἱ δὲ διὰ ταῦτα μαχόμενοι μάχιμοι μέν, οὐκ ἀνδρεῖοι δέ· οὐ γὰρ διὰ τὸ καλὸν οὐδ᾽ ὡς ὁ λόγος, ἀλλὰ διὰ πάθος· παραπλήσιον δ᾽ ἔχουσί τι.

οὐδὲ δὴ οἱ εὐέλπιδες ὄντες ἀνδρεῖοι· διὰ γὰρ τὸ πολλάκις καὶ πολλοὺς νενικηκέναι θαρροῦσιν ἐν τοῖς κινδύνοις· παρόμοιοι δέ, ὅτι ἄμφω θαρραλέοι· ἀλλ᾽ οἱ μὲν ἀνδρεῖοι διὰ τὰ πρότερον εἰρημένα θαρραλέοι, οἳ δὲ διὰ τὸ οἴεσθαι κράτιστοι εἶναι καὶ μηθὲν ἂν παθεῖν. . . . ὅταν δὲ αὐτοῖς μὴ συμβῇ τὰ τοιαῦτα, φεύγουσιν· ἀνδρείου δ᾽ ἦν τὰ φοβερὰ ἀνθρώπῳ ὄντα καὶ φαινόμενα ὑπομένειν,

natural form, and if it also includes choice and purpose, it really is bravery. Also, people are pained when they are angry and get pleasure from exacting revenge. People who attack for these reasons are spoiling for a fight, but not brave. They do not fight because it is noble, or because thinking tells them to do it; they fight because their passion is enflamed. Still, their condition is close to bravery.

Soldiers who are confident of victory aren't brave, either. They are bold in dangerous situations because they have won many victories and defeated many opponents in the past. They closely resemble the brave, in that both types are emboldened. But the brave are emboldened for the reasons already mentioned, while these type are bold because they think they are stronger than their opponents and won't be harmed. . . . When it turns out that this is not how things are for them, they flee. But to be brave you must stand firm in the face of what really frightens you, and would frighten anyone, and you

ὅτι καλὸν καὶ αἰσχρὸν τὸ μή. διὸ καὶ ἀνδρειοτέρου δοκεῖ εἶναι τὸ ἐν τοῖς αἰφνιδίοις φόβοις ἄφοβον καὶ ἀτάραχον εἶναι ἢ ἐν τοῖς προδήλοις· ἀπὸ ἕξεως γὰρ μᾶλλον ἦν, ὅτι ἧττον ἐκ παρασκευῆς· τὰ προφανῆ μὲν γὰρ κἂν ἐκ λογισμοῦ καὶ λόγου τις προέλοιτο, τὰ δ᾽ ἐξαίφνης κατὰ τὴν ἕξιν.

ἀνδρεῖοι δὲ φαίνονται καὶ οἱ ἀγνοοῦντες, καὶ εἰσὶν οὐ πόρρω τῶν εὐελπίδων, χείρους δ᾽ ὅσῳ ἀξίωμα οὐδὲν ἔχουσιν, ἐκεῖνοι δέ. διὸ καὶ μένουσί τινα χρόνον· οἱ δ᾽ ἠπατημένοι, ἐὰν γνῶσιν ὅτι ἕτερον ἢ ὑποπτεύσωσι, φεύγουσιν· ὅπερ οἱ Ἀργεῖοι ἔπαθον περιπεσόντες τοῖς Λάκωσιν ὡς Σικυωνίοις.

οἵ τε δὴ ἀνδρεῖοι εἴρηνται ποῖοί τινες, καὶ οἱ δοκοῦντες ἀνδρεῖοι.

must do so because it is noble to stand your ground, and shameful not to. That is why it seems braver to be fearless and undisturbed in sudden alarms than when the danger is clear in advance. Your reaction is more from your disposition to the extent that it not prepared in advance. When the danger can be foreseen, your choice might also be based on calculation and thinking. But when reacting on the spot, you act from your disposition.

Soldiers who fight in ignorance also appear to be brave. They are not far removed from those who are confident of victory, but they are worse, in that soldiers confident of victory have something worthy about them, which is why they do hold ranks for a while. By contrast, mistaken fighters flee as soon as they realize that things are not as they had supposed. That is what happened when the Argives attacked the Spartans, thinking they were Sicyonians.[17]

We have now stated what sort of people are brave, and what sort only seem to be brave.

[3.10] Μετὰ δὲ ταύτην περὶ σωφροσύνης λέγω-
μεν· δοκοῦσι γὰρ τῶν ἀλόγων μερῶν αὗται εἶναι
αἱ ἀρεταί. ὅτι μὲν οὖν μεσότης ἐστὶ περὶ ἡδονὰς ἡ
σωφροσύνη, εἴρηται ἡμῖν· . . . περὶ ποίας οὖν τῶν

In chapter 9 Aristotle concludes his account of bravery with a discussion of the pleasures and pains involved in brave action.

FOOD, DRINK, AND SEX

Aristotle now turns to discuss self-discipline in the pursuit and enjoyment of bodily pleasures. His name for this virtue is SŌPHROSUNĒ, which in ordinary Greek encompasses soundness of mind, decorum, self-control, resistance to temptation or provocation, and the ability to keep a cool head and maintain your resolve under pressure. Aristotle narrows the range of this virtue to the domain of bodily pleasures, and the translation uses "self-discipline" in a similarly restricted sense.

[3.10] Next after bravery, let us discuss *self-discipline*, since these seem to be the virtues of the unthinking parts. Self-discipline is a mean in matters of pleasure, as we have said. . . . Let us now indicate the sorts of pleasures it concerns.

ἡδονῶν, νῦν ἀφορίσωμεν. διῃρήσθωσαν δὴ αἱ ψυχικαὶ καὶ αἱ σωματικαί, οἷον φιλοτιμία φιλομάθεια· ἑκάτερος γὰρ τούτων χαίρει, οὗ φιλητικός ἐστιν, οὐδὲν πάσχοντος τοῦ σώματος, ἀλλὰ μᾶλλον τῆς διανοίας· οἱ δὲ περὶ τὰς τοιαύτας ἡδονὰς οὔτε σώφρονες οὔτε ἀκόλαστοι λέγονται. ὁμοίως δ' οὐδ' οἱ περὶ τὰς ἄλλας ὅσαι μὴ σωματικαί εἰσιν· . . .

περὶ δὲ τὰς σωματικὰς εἴη ἂν ἡ σωφροσύνη, οὐ πάσας δὲ οὐδὲ ταύτας· οἱ γὰρ χαίροντες τοῖς διὰ τῆς ὄψεως, οἷον χρώμασι καὶ σχήμασι καὶ γραφῇ, οὔτε σώφρονες οὔτε ἀκόλαστοι λέγονται· καίτοι δόξειεν ἂν εἶναι καὶ ὡς δεῖ χαίρειν καὶ τούτοις, καὶ καθ' ὑπερβολὴν καὶ ἔλλειψιν. ὁμοίως δὲ καὶ ἐν τοῖς περὶ τὴν ἀκοήν· τοὺς γὰρ ὑπερβεβλημένως χαίροντας μέλεσιν ἢ ὑποκρίσει οὐθεὶς ἀκολάστους λέγει, . . . οὐδὲ τοὺς περὶ τὴν ὀσμήν, πλὴν κατὰ συμβεβηκός· τοὺς γὰρ χαίροντας μήλων ἢ ῥόδων ἢ θυμιαμάτων ὀσμαῖς

Pleasures of the soul[18] are distinct from those of the body. Consider, for example, love of honor and love of learning. Neither of these has any effect on the body when it rejoices in its object; it is the intellect that is affected. No one is called self-disciplined or self-indulgent with respect to these pleasures, or indeed regarding any pleasure that is not bodily. . . .

So self-discipline is about bodily pleasures. But not all of them. For example, it is not about the pleasures you take in objects of sight, such as colors and figures, or a painting. People who enjoy these are not called self-disciplined or self-indulgent, even though there would seem to be appropriate, excessive, and deficient ways of enjoying them. The same goes for pleasures of hearing, since no one would be called self-indulgent for taking excessive pleasure in listening to songs or dramatic recitations. . . . It is not about the pleasures of smell, either, except incidentally. We don't call people self-indulgent for delighting in the scent of apples or roses or

οὐ λέγομεν ἀκολάστους, ἀλλὰ μᾶλλον τοὺς μύρων ἢ ὄψων· χαίρουσι γὰρ τούτοις οἱ ἀκόλαστοι, ὅτι διὰ τούτων ἀνάμνησις γίνεται αὐτοῖς τῶν ἐπιθυμημάτων . . .

περὶ τὰς τοιαύτας δ' ἡδονὰς ἡ σωφροσύνη καὶ ἡ ἀκολασία ἐστὶν ὧν καὶ τὰ λοιπὰ ζῷα κοινωνεῖ. . . . αὗται δ' εἰσὶν ἁφὴ καὶ γεῦσις. φαίνονται δὲ καὶ τῇ γεύσει ἐπὶ μικρὸν ἢ οὐθὲν χρῆσθαι· τῆς γὰρ γεύσεώς ἐστιν ἡ κρίσις τῶν χυμῶν, ὅπερ ποιοῦσιν οἱ τοὺς οἴνους δοκιμάζοντες καὶ τὰ ὄψα ἀρτύοντες· οὐ πάνυ δὲ χαίρουσι τούτοις, ἢ οὐχ οἵ γε ἀκόλαστοι, ἀλλὰ τῇ ἀπολαύσει, ἢ γίνεται πᾶσα δι' ἁφῆς καὶ ἐν σιτίοις καὶ ἐν ποτοῖς καὶ τοῖς ἀφροδισίοις λεγομένοις. διὸ καὶ ηὔξατό τις ὀψοφάγος ὢν τὸν φάρυγγα αὐτῷ μακρότερον γεράνου γενέσθαι, ὡς ἡδόμενος τῇ ἁφῇ . . . τὸ δὴ τοιούτοις χαίρειν καὶ μάλιστα ἀγαπᾶν θηριῶδες. καὶ γὰρ αἱ ἐλευθεριώταται τῶν διὰ τῆς ἁφῆς ἡδονῶν ἀφῄρηνται, οἷον αἱ ἐν τοῖς γυμνασίοις διὰ τρίψεως καὶ τῆς θερμασίας γινόμεναι·

incense. We are more likely to do so if they delight in the scent of myrrh or of meat, since a self-indulgent person will take pleasure in these scents, because they remind him of the object he craves. . . .

Self-discipline and self-indulgence concern the sorts of pleasures that we have in common with other animals. . . . Those are the pleasures of touch and taste, although taste has at most a small role to play, since tasting is a matter of discriminating flavors—what you do when evaluating wines, or seasoning meat. It is not exactly *taste* that you take pleasure in if you are self-indulgent. It is the feeling of gratification, and this comes entirely through *touch*, whether in eating or in drinking or in sex. That is why a certain gourmand prayed for his throat to grow longer than a crane's, he enjoyed touch so much! . . . To delight in such things and to be especially fond of them is brutish. We don't include here the most cultivated pleasures of touch, such as those from rubbing and heating

οὐ γὰρ περὶ πᾶν τὸ σῶμα ἡ τοῦ ἀκολάστου ἁφή, ἀλλὰ περί τινα μέρη.

[3.11] Τῶν δ᾽ ἐπιθυμιῶν αἳ μὲν κοιναὶ δοκοῦσιν εἶναι, αἳ δ᾽ ἴδιοι καὶ ἐπίθετοι· οἷον ἡ μὲν τῆς τροφῆς φυσική· πᾶς γὰρ ἐπιθυμεῖ ὁ ἐνδεὴς ξηρᾶς ἢ ὑγρᾶς τροφῆς, ὁτὲ δὲ ἀμφοῖν, καὶ εὐνῆς, . . . τὸ δὲ τοιᾶσδε ἢ τοιᾶσδε, οὐκέτι πᾶς, οὐδὲ τῶν αὐτῶν. διὸ φαίνεται ἡμέτερον εἶναι. οὐ μὴν ἀλλ᾽ ἔχει γέ τι καὶ φυσικόν· ἕτερα γὰρ ἑτέροις ἐστὶν ἡδέα, καὶ ἔνια πᾶσιν ἡδίω τῶν τυχόντων. ἐν μὲν οὖν ταῖς φυσικαῖς ἐπιθυμίαις ὀλίγοι ἁμαρτάνουσι καὶ ἐφ᾽ ἕν, ἐπὶ τὸ πλεῖον· τὸ γὰρ ἐσθίειν τὰ τυχόντα ἢ πίνειν ἕως ἂν ὑπερπλησθῇ, ὑπερβάλλειν ἐστὶ τὸ κατὰ φύσιν τῷ πλήθει· ἀναπλήρωσις γὰρ τῆς ἐνδείας ἡ φυσικὴ ἐπιθυμία. διὸ λέγονται οὗτοι γαστρίμαργοι, ὡς παρὰ τὸ δέον πληροῦντες αὐτήν. . . .

in the gymnasium. Self-indulgence isn't about touching just any part of the body, only certain parts.

[3.11] Some appetites seem to be commonly shared, while others are individual and acquired. The appetite for food, for example, is natural, since any creature, when in need, feels an appetite for food or drink, sometimes for both, and for sleep. . . . But not everyone has this or that sort of appetite, or appetite for the same things; these seem to be our own doing. Still, there is an element of nature, since different things are pleasant to different creatures, and there are some things that all creatures find more pleasant than the ordinary. Now, few people go wrong in their natural appetites, and if they do, it is in the direction of too much. To eat or drink until you are overfull is to exceed the natural limit, since a natural appetite is for replenishing what you lack. That's why people who do this are called gluttons: they fill up beyond the point of need. . . .

περὶ δὲ τὰς ἰδίας τῶν ἡδονῶν πολλοὶ καὶ πολ-
λαχῶς ἁμαρτάνουσιν. τῶν γὰρ φιλοτοιούτων λε-
γομένων ἢ τῷ χαίρειν οἷς μὴ δεῖ, ἢ τῷ μᾶλλον ἢ
ὡς οἱ πολλοί, ἢ μὴ ὡς δεῖ, κατὰ πάντα δ' οἱ ἀκόλαστοι ὑπερβάλλουσιν· καὶ γὰρ χαίρουσιν ἐνίοις οἷς
οὐ δεῖ (μισητὰ γάρ), καὶ εἴ τισι δεῖ χαίρειν τῶν
τοιούτων, μᾶλλον ἢ δεῖ καὶ ἢ ὡς οἱ πολλοὶ χαίρουσιν. ἡ μὲν οὖν περὶ τὰς ἡδονὰς ὑπερβολὴ ὅτι ἀκολασία καὶ ψεκτόν, δῆλον·

περὶ δὲ τὰς λύπας οὐχ ὥσπερ ἐπὶ τῆς ἀνδρείας
τῷ ὑπομένειν λέγεται σώφρων οὐδ' ἀκόλαστος
τῷ μή, ἀλλ' ὁ μὲν ἀκόλαστος τῷ λυπεῖσθαι μᾶλλον ἢ δεῖ ὅτι τῶν ἡδέων οὐ τυγχάνει . . . , ὁ δὲ
σώφρων τῷ μὴ λυπεῖσθαι τῇ ἀπουσίᾳ καὶ τῷ ἀπέχεσθαι τοῦ ἡδέος. Ὁ μὲν οὖν ἀκόλαστος ἐπιθυμεῖ

In matters of individual pleasures, there are many ways to go wrong, and most of us do. For example, there are people who get called "lovers" of a thing[19] if they enjoy something they shouldn't, or enjoy a thing more than they should, or more than most people do, or not in the way they should. Self-indulgent people go to excess in all these ways. They enjoy things that are wrong to enjoy; or it is right to enjoy *some* such things, but these people enjoy them more than is right, or more than most people do. Going to excess in matters of pleasure is clearly self-indulgent and blameworthy.

As for pains, it is unlike the case of bravery; you are not called self-disciplined or self-indulgent based on whether you endure pains or give in to them. You are called are self-indulgent for being more pained than you should at missing out on pleasant opportunities . . . and you are called self-disciplined for not being pained at the absence of pleasures, or at abstaining from something pleasant. Self-indulgent people

τῶν ἡδέων πάντων ἢ τῶν μάλιστα, καὶ ἄγεται ὑπὸ
τῆς ἐπιθυμίας ὥστε ἀντὶ τῶν ἄλλων ταῦθ᾽ αἱρεῖ-
σθαι· διὸ καὶ λυπεῖται καὶ ἀποτυγχάνων καὶ ἐπι-
θυμῶν· μετὰ λύπης γὰρ ἡ ἐπιθυμία· . . .

ἐλλείποντες δὲ τὰ περὶ τὰς ἡδονὰς καὶ ἧττον ἢ
δεῖ χαίροντες οὐ πάνυ γίνονται· οὐ γὰρ ἀνθρω-
πική ἐστιν ἡ τοιαύτη ἀναισθησία· καὶ γὰρ τὰ λοιπὰ
ζῷα διακρίνει τὰ βρώματα, καὶ τοῖς μὲν χαίρει τοῖς
δ᾽ οὔ· εἰ δέ τῳ μηδέν ἐστιν ἡδὺ μηδὲ διαφέρει ἕτερον ἑτέρου, πόρρω ἂν εἴη τοῦ ἄνθρωπος εἶναι·
οὐ τέτευχε δ᾽ ὁ τοιοῦτος ὀνόματος διὰ τὸ μὴ πάνυ
γίνεσθαι.

ὁ δὲ σώφρων μέσως μὲν περὶ ταῦτ᾽ ἔχει· οὔτε
γὰρ ἥδεται οἷς μάλιστα ὁ ἀκόλαστος, ἀλλὰ μᾶλλον δυσχεραίνει, οὐδ᾽ ὅλως οἷς μὴ δεῖ οὐδὲ σφόδρα τοιούτῳ οὐδενί, οὔτ᾽ ἀπόντων λυπεῖται οὐδ᾽

have an appetite for all pleasures, or for especially strong ones, and appetite leads them to choose these pleasures over any alternative. As a result they are pained both when they miss out on the pleasure and when they have an appetite for it, since appetite involves pain. . . .

Falling short in matters of pleasure and enjoying them less than you should is not very common. Such impassivity is not human. Even other animals discriminate between different types of food, taking pleasure in some, not in others. People who found nothing pleasant, and preferred nothing to anything else, would fall well short of being human. There is no name for them, since there are barely any of them.

People with self-discipline are disposed to strike the middle course in these matters. For example, they are disgusted rather than pleased by what self-indulgent people enjoy the most. In general, they do not enjoy things they should not, or enjoy anything in this domain intensely.

ἐπιθυμεῖ, ἢ μετρίως, οὐδὲ μᾶλλον ἢ δεῖ, οὐδ' ὅτε μὴ δεῖ, οὐδ' ὅλως τῶν τοιούτων οὐδέν· ὅσα δὲ πρὸς ὑγίειάν ἐστιν ἢ πρὸς εὐεξίαν ἡδέα ὄντα, τούτων ὀρέξεται μετρίως καὶ ὡς δεῖ, καὶ τῶν ἄλλων ἡδέων μὴ ἐμποδίων τούτοις ὄντων ἢ παρὰ τὸ καλὸν ἢ ὑπὲρ τὴν οὐσίαν. ὁ γὰρ οὕτως ἔχων μᾶλλον ἀγαπᾷ τὰς τοιαύτας ἡδονὰς τῆς ἀξίας· ὁ δὲ σώφρων οὐ τοιοῦτος, ἀλλ' ὡς ὁ ὀρθὸς λόγος.

[3.12] . . . διὸ δεῖ τοῦ σώφρονος τὸ ἐπιθυμητικὸν συμφωνεῖν τῷ λόγῳ· σκοπὸς γὰρ ἀμφοῖν τὸ

In the absence of such pleasures, they do not feel pain or longing—or their feelings will be properly measured (not too much, or at the wrong time, and so forth). They *will* have desires for pleasures that are conducive to health and fitness (in due measure and as they should), and for other pleasures, provided they do not impede health or fitness or go beyond what is decent or what they can afford. Otherwise, their liking for such pleasures would exceed what the pleasures are worth. A self-disciplined person, however, reacts as correct thinking prescribes.

In the final chapter of book 3, Aristotle compares cowardice and self-indulgence and describes the psychological structure of self-discipline: the thinking part of the soul is in charge, and the appetitive and desiring part of the soul follows its lead.

[3.12] . . . If you have self-discipline, your appetitive part should follow your thinking part. Both parts will have decency as their target, and

καλόν, καὶ ἐπιθυμεῖ ὁ σώφρων ὧν δεῖ καὶ ὡς δεῖ καὶ ὅτε· οὕτω δὲ τάττει καὶ ὁ λόγος.

ταῦτ᾽ οὖν ἡμῖν εἰρήσθω περὶ σωφροσύνης. . . .

[4.1] Λέγωμεν δ᾽ ἑξῆς περὶ ἐλευθεριότητος. δοκεῖ δὴ εἶναι ἡ περὶ χρήματα μεσότης· ἐπαινεῖται γὰρ ὁ ἐλευθέριος οὐκ ἐν τοῖς πολεμικοῖς, οὐδ᾽ ἐν οἷς ὁ σώφρων, οὐδ᾽ αὖ ἐν ταῖς κρίσεσιν, ἀλλὰ περὶ δόσιν χρημάτων καὶ λῆψιν, μᾶλλον δ᾽ ἐν τῇ δόσει. χρήματα δὲ λέγομεν πάντα ὅσων ἡ ἀξία νομίσματι μετρεῖται. ἔστι δὲ καὶ ἡ ἀσωτία καὶ ἡ ἀνελευθερία περὶ χρήματα ὑπερβολαὶ καὶ ἐλλείψεις· καὶ τὴν

your appetites will be for the right things, in the right way, and at the right time—that is, as thinking tells us.

Let this be our account of self-discipline.

Book 4 continues Aristotle's treatment of individual virtues and vices of character. It opens with, GENEROSITY, whose domain is money: how we acquire it, and more importantly, how we use it—especially to whom we give it.

Personal Finance

[4.1] Next let us discuss *generosity*, which seems to be a mean in matters of wealth. It is not for conduct on the battlefield, in matters of self-discipline, or on a jury that generous people are praised; it is for giving away and taking in wealth, but more for giving. (By wealth we mean anything whose value is measured in money.) In managing your finances, it is both excessive and deficient to be *extravagant* or

μὲν ἀνελευθερίαν προσάπτομεν ἀεὶ τοῖς μᾶλλον ἢ δεῖ περὶ χρήματα σπουδάζουσι, τὴν δ' ἀσωτίαν ἐπιφέρομεν ἐνίοτε συμπλέκοντες· . . . βούλεται γὰρ ἄσωτος εἶναι ὁ ἓν κακὸν ἔχων, τὸ φθείρειν τὴν οὐσίαν· . . .

Αἱ δὲ κατ' ἀρετὴν πράξεις καλαὶ καὶ τοῦ καλοῦ ἕνεκα. καὶ ὁ ἐλευθέριος οὖν δώσει τοῦ καλοῦ ἕνεκα καὶ ὀρθῶς· οἷς γὰρ δεῖ καὶ ὅσα καὶ ὅτε, καὶ τἆλλα ὅσα ἕπεται τῇ ὀρθῇ δόσει· καὶ ταῦτα ἡδέως ἢ ἀλύπως· τὸ γὰρ κατ' ἀρετὴν ἡδὺ ἢ ἄλυπον,. . . . οὐδ' ὁ λυπηρῶς· μᾶλλον γὰρ ἕλοιτ' ἂν τὰ χρήματα τῆς καλῆς πράξεως, τοῦτο δ' οὐκ ἐλευθερίου.

οὐδὲ λήψεται δὲ ὅθεν μὴ δεῖ· οὐ γάρ ἐστι τοῦ μὴ τιμῶντος τὰ χρήματα ἡ τοιαύτη λῆψις. οὐκ ἂν εἴη δὲ οὐδ' αἰτητικός· οὐ γάρ ἐστι τοῦ εὖ ποιοῦντος

moneygrubbing. We call people *moneygrubbing*
if they take wealth more seriously than they
should. When we charge someone with extravagance, we sometimes confuse it with other
things, . . . but extravagance involves one evil in
particular: ruin of your livelihood. . . .

Virtuous actions are the decent thing to do
and are performed for that reason. That is, generous people have decency in mind when they
give and will give correctly: to whom, and as
much as, and when they should—along with all
the other dimensions of correct giving. They
will also do so with pleasure, or without pain,
since the activity of virtue is pleasant (or pain-
less). . . . You are not generous if it pains you to
give, since you are likely to choose wealth over
decency, and that is not what a generous person
does.

Generous people won't accept money from
inappropriate sources, either, since that is not
what you do if you don't value wealth. They are
not even inclined to ask for it, since people who

εὐχερῶς εὐεργετεῖσθαι. . . . ἐλευθερίου δ᾽ ἐστὶ σφόδρα καὶ τὸ ὑπερβάλλειν ἐν τῇ δόσει, ὥστε καταλείπειν ἑαυτῷ ἐλάττω· τὸ γὰρ μὴ βλέπειν ἐφ᾽ ἑαυτὸν ἐλευθερίου. κατὰ τὴν οὐσίαν δ᾽ ἡ ἐλευθεριότης λέγεται· οὐ γὰρ ἐν τῷ πλήθει τῶν διδομένων τὸ ἐλευθέριον, ἀλλ᾽ ἐν τῇ τοῦ διδόντος ἕξει, αὕτη δὲ κατὰ τὴν οὐσίαν δίδωσιν. οὐθὲν δὴ κωλύει ἐλευθεριώτερον εἶναι τὸν τὰ ἐλάττω διδόντα, ἐὰν ἀπ᾽ ἐλαττόνων διδῷ. . . .

καὶ εὐκοινώνητος δ᾽ ἐστὶν ὁ ἐλευθέριος εἰς χρήματα· δύναται γὰρ ἀδικεῖσθαι, μὴ τιμῶν γε τὰ χρήματα, καὶ μᾶλλον ἀχθόμενος εἴ τι δέον μὴ ἀνάλωσεν ἢ λυπούμενος εἰ μὴ δέον τι ἀνάλωσεν, . . .

εἴρηται δὴ ἡμῖν ὅτι ὑπερβολαὶ καὶ ἐλλείψεις εἰσὶν ἡ ἀσωτία καὶ ἡ ἀνελευθερία, καὶ ἐν δυσίν, ἐν δόσει καὶ λήψει· καὶ τὴν δαπάνην γὰρ εἰς τὴν δόσιν τίθεμεν. ἡ μὲν οὖν ἀσωτία τῷ διδόναι καὶ

perform good services do not find it easy to receive them. . . . They will give abundantly, even
to excess, leaving themselves a lesser share—
since it is characteristic of generous people not
to be looking out for their own interests. (What
counts as generous depends on your resources;
a gift is generous not in virtue of its size, but in
virtue to the giver's disposition, which is to give
in line with their resources. It is possible to be
more generous while giving a smaller amount,
if you are giving from lesser resources.) . . .

A generous person is also easy to do business
with. They can be taken advantage of, since they
do not value wealth, and are more upset if they
have failed to pay out what they should have
than if they have paid out what they did not
have to. . . .

We have stated that *extravagance* and *moneygrubbing* are excessive and deficient in both
activities—giving away and taking in wealth (we
include spending under giving). *Extravagant*
people go to excess in giving and refusing to

μὴ λαμβάνειν ὑπερβάλλει, τῷ δὲ λαμβάνειν ἐλλείπει, ἡ δ᾽ ἀνελευθερία τῷ διδόναι μὲν ἐλλείπει,
τῷ λαμβάνειν δ᾽ ὑπερβάλλει, πλὴν ἐν μικροῖς. τὰ
μὲν οὖν τῆς ἀσωτίας οὐ πάνυ συνδυάζεται· οὐ γὰρ
ῥᾴδιον μηδαμόθεν λαμβάνοντα πᾶσι διδόναι· ταχέως γὰρ ἐπιλείπει ἡ οὐσία τοὺς ἰδιώτας διδό-
ντας, οἵπερ καὶ δοκοῦσιν ἄσωτοι εἶναι· ἐπεὶ ὅ γε
τοιοῦτος δόξειεν ἂν οὐ μικρῷ βελτίων εἶναι τοῦ
ἀνελευθέρου.... διὸ καὶ δοκεῖ οὐκ εἶναι φαῦλος
τὸ ἦθος· οὐ γὰρ μοχθηροῦ οὐδ᾽ ἀγεννοῦς τὸ
ὑπερβάλλειν διδόντα καὶ μὴ λαμβάνοντα, ἠλι-
θίου δέ. ὁ δὲ τοῦτον τὸν τρόπον ἄσωτος πολὺ
δοκεῖ βελτίων τοῦ ἀνελευθέρου εἶναι διά τε τὰ
εἰρημένα, καὶ ὅτι ὃ μὲν ὠφελεῖ πολλούς, ὃ δὲ
οὐθένα, ἀλλ᾽ οὐδ᾽ αὑτόν....

καὶ διατείνει δ᾽ ἐπὶ πολύ, καὶ πολυειδές ἐστιν·
πολλοὶ γὰρ τρόποι δοκοῦσι τῆς ἀνελευθερίας
εἶναι. ἐν δυσὶ γὰρ οὖσα, τῇ τ᾽ ἐλλείψει τῆς δόσεως
καὶ τῇ ὑπερβολῇ τῆς λήψεως, οὐ πᾶσιν ὁλόκληρος

take, and they are deficient at taking. *Money-grubbers* give too seldom and take in too often, except in small matters. The two aspects of *extravagance* are not easily combined, because it is difficult to give to everyone while taking in from nowhere. If you give away your own property, you will quickly run out. And this does seem to be extravagant, even if considerably better than moneygrubbing. . . . It doesn't impress us as a defect of character, since giving to excess without taking any in is not vicious or ill bred, just simpleminded. People who are extravagant in this way seem a lot better than moneygrubbers—both for the reasons we have given and because they help a lot of people, while *moneygrubbers* help no one, not even themselves. . . .

Moneygrubbing is more widespread and varied than *extravagance*, since it comes in many forms. Its two main features are deficient giving and excessive taking, although both faults are not present in all cases. Sometimes they occur

παραγίνεται, ἀλλ' ἐνίοτε χωρίζεται, καὶ οἳ μὲν τῇ λήψει ὑπερβάλλουσιν, οἳ δὲ τῇ δόσει ἐλλείπουσιν. οἱ μὲν γὰρ ἐν ταῖς τοιαύταις προσηγορίαις οἷον φειδωλοὶ γλίσχροι κίμβικες, πάντες τῇ δόσει ἐλλείπουσι, τῶν δ' ἀλλοτρίων οὐκ ἐφίενται οὐδὲ βούλονται λαμβάνειν, οἳ μὲν διά τινα ἐπιείκειαν καὶ εὐλάβειαν τῶν αἰσχρῶν (δοκοῦσι γὰρ ἔνιοι ἢ φασί γε διὰ τοῦτο φυλάττειν, ἵνα μή ποτ' ἀναγκασθῶσιν αἰσχρόν τι πρᾶξαι· τούτων δὲ καὶ ὁ κυμινοπρίστης καὶ πᾶς ὁ τοιοῦτος· ὠνόμασται δ' ἀπὸ τῆς ὑπερβολῆς τοῦ μηδὲν ἂν δοῦναι)· . . .

οἳ δ' αὖ κατὰ τὴν λῆψιν ὑπερβάλλουσι τῷ πάντοθεν λαμβάνειν καὶ πᾶν, οἷον οἱ τὰς ἀνελευθέρους ἐργασίας ἐργαζόμενοι, πορνοβοσκοὶ καὶ πάντες οἱ τοιοῦτοι, καὶ τοκισταὶ κατὰ μικρὰ καὶ ἐπὶ πολλῷ. πάντες γὰρ οὗτοι ὅθεν οὐ δεῖ λαμβάνουσι, καὶ ὁπόσον οὐ δεῖ. κοινὸν δ' ἐπ' αὐτοῖς ἡ αἰσχροκέρδεια φαίνεται· πάντες γὰρ ἕνεκα κέρδους, καὶ τούτου μικροῦ, ὀνείδη ὑπομένουσιν. . . .

separately, with some *moneygrubbers* taking in excessively and others falling short in giving. People who get called such things as *miser*, *tightwad*, or *skinflint* fall short in giving, although they don't covet and won't take what belongs to others. For some of them, it is because of a kind of decency, a concern to avoid disgrace. (It seems they conserve their resources so that they will never be forced to do anything shameful—or so they say.) These include *seed splitters* and their ilk; the label reflects their excessive reluctance to give anything away. . . .

Some people who go to excess in taking in money are willing to exploit every opportunity to acquire it, no matter what the source. They practice sordid trades such as brothel keeping, or they lend out small sums at high interest. All of them take in wealth from the wrong sources, or beyond what is right. What they clearly have in common is shameful profiteering. All of them put up with disgrace in order to make a profit, even a small one. . . . *Moneygrubbers* include

ὁ μέντοι κυβευτὴς καὶ ὁ λωποδύτης καὶ ὁ λῃστὴς
τῶν ἀνελευθέρων εἰσίν· αἰσχροκερδεῖς γάρ. κέρδους γὰρ ἕνεκα ἀμφότεροι πραγματεύονται καὶ
ὀνείδη ὑπομένουσιν, καὶ οἳ μὲν κινδύνους τοὺς με-
γίστους ἕνεκα τοῦ λήμματος, οἳ δ᾽ ἀπὸ τῶν φίλων
κερδαίνουσιν, οἷς δεῖ διδόναι. ἀμφότεροι δὴ ὅθεν
οὐ δεῖ κερδαίνειν βουλόμενοι αἰσχροκερδεῖς· καὶ
πᾶσαι δὴ αἱ τοιαῦται λήψεις ἀνελεύθεροι.

εἰκότως δὲ τῇ ἐλευθεριότητι ἀνελευθερία ἐναν-
τίον λέγεται· μεῖζόν τε γάρ ἐστι κακὸν τῆς ἀσωτίας, καὶ μᾶλλον ἐπὶ ταύτην ἁμαρτάνουσιν ἢ κατὰ
τὴν λεχθεῖσαν ἀσωτίαν. περὶ μὲν οὖν ἐλευθεριότητος καὶ τῶν ἀντικειμένων κακιῶν τοσαῦτ᾽
εἰρήσθω.

gamblers, and also highway robbers and pirates. Both groups are shameful profiteers, willing to incur disgrace as long as they can profit from plying their trades. The latter risk extreme dangers in order to secure their criminal gains. The former make a profit off the very people to whom they should be giving—that is, their friends. Since both groups are willing to make a profit where they shouldn't, they are shameful profiteers. All such ways of acquiring wealth are *moneygrubbing*.

People say that *moneygrubbing* is the opposite of generosity, and that makes sense. It is a greater evil than *extravagance*, and people are more likely to err in its direction than in the direction of extravagance, as we have described it. So much then, for our discussion of *generosity* and its opposing vices.

In chapter 2, Aristotle describes PHILANTHROPY *(generosity on a larger scale). In chapters 3 and 4 he presents two virtues concerning honor. The*

[4.5] Πραότης δ᾽ ἐστὶ μεσότης περὶ ὀργάς·
ἀνωνύμου δ᾽ ὄντος τοῦ μέσου, σχεδὸν δὲ καὶ τῶν
ἄκρων, ἐπὶ τὸ μέσον τὴν πραότητα φέρομεν, πρὸς
τὴν ἔλλειψιν ἀποκλίνουσαν, ἀνώνυμον οὖσαν.
ἡ δ᾽ ὑπερβολὴ ὀργιλότης τις λέγοιτ᾽ ἄν. τὸ μὲν γὰρ
πάθος ἐστὶν ὀργή, τὰ δ᾽ ἐμποιοῦντα πολλὰ καὶ
διαφέροντα. ὁ μὲν οὖν ἐφ᾽ οἷς δεῖ καὶ οἷς δεῖ ὀρ-
γιζόμενος, ἔτι δὲ καὶ ὡς δεῖ καὶ ὅτε καὶ ὅσον
χρόνον, ἐπαινεῖται· ... βούλεται γὰρ ὁ πρᾶος
ἀτάραχος εἶναι καὶ μὴ ἄγεσθαι ὑπὸ τοῦ πάθους,
ἀλλ᾽ ὡς ἂν ὁ λόγος τάξῃ, οὕτω καὶ ἐπὶ τούτοις καὶ

first, MAGNANIMITY, *concerns the pursuit of great honors such as high office. The second, which lacks a name, concerns smaller scale honors and offices. In chapter 5, Aristotle turns to the domain of anger.*

ANGER MANAGEMENT

[4.5] Even temper is the intermediate in matters of anger. There is no name for the mean—and hardly for the extremes either—but we will use *even temper* for the mean (even though that label might suggest the deficiency, which also lacks a name). You might call the excess *hot temper*, since what you feel is temper, although many different things provoke it. People are praised if they get angry for the right reasons and at the right people, as well as how and when they should, and for the right length of time. . . . Being even tempered means not being agitated or led about by passion. It means you follow the direction of thought in what you get upset about,

ἐπὶ τοσοῦτον χρόνον χαλεπαίνειν· ἁμαρτάνειν δὲ δοκεῖ μᾶλλον ἐπὶ τὴν ἔλλειψιν· οὐ γὰρ τιμωρητικὸς ὁ πρᾶος, ἀλλὰ μᾶλλον συγγνωμονικός.

ἡ δ’ ἔλλειψις, εἴτ’ ἀοργησία τίς ἐστιν εἴθ’ ὅ τι δή ποτε, ψέγεται. οἱ γὰρ μὴ ὀργιζόμενοι ἐφ’ οἷς δεῖ ἠλίθιοι δοκοῦσιν εἶναι, καὶ οἱ μὴ ὡς δεῖ μηδ’ ὅτε μηδ’ οἷς δεῖ· δοκεῖ γὰρ οὐκ αἰσθάνεσθαι οὐδὲ λυπεῖσθαι, μὴ ὀργιζόμενός τε οὐκ εἶναι ἀμυντικός, τὸ δὲ προπηλακιζόμενον ἀνέχεσθαι καὶ τοὺς οἰκείους περιορᾶν ἀνδραποδῶδες.

ἡ δ’ ὑπερβολὴ κατὰ πάντα μὲν γίνεται (καὶ γὰρ οἷς οὐ δεῖ, καὶ ἐφ’ οἷς οὐ δεῖ, καὶ μᾶλλον ἢ δεῖ, καὶ θᾶττον, καὶ πλείω χρόνον), . . . οἱ μὲν οὖν ὀργίλοι ταχέως μὲν ὀργίζονται καὶ οἷς οὐ δεῖ καὶ ἐφ’ οἷς οὐ δεῖ καὶ μᾶλλον ἢ δεῖ, παύονται δὲ ταχέως· ὃ καὶ βέλτιστον ἔχουσιν. συμβαίνει δ’ αὐτοῖς τοῦτο,

and how long you remain upset. Even-tempered people seem more likely to err in the direction of deficiency, since they tend to be forgiving rather than vengeful.

Deficiency in these matters gets blamed, whether it is not getting angry at all, or whatever. People seem to be naive if they fail to get angry about things that should anger them, and if they don't get angry in the right way, at the right time, and at the right people. When you don't get angry, it seems you don't notice the offense and are not upset about it, and are unlikely to strike back. But it is slavish to put up with being insulted, or look on while your family is being insulted.

Anger can be excessive in all these dimensions. It can be directed at the wrong people, or about the wrong things, or it can arise faster or last longer than it should. . . . Hot-tempered people get angry quickly—at the wrong people and about the wrong things and more intensely than they should—but they stop quickly too,

ὅτι οὐ κατέχουσι τὴν ὀργὴν ἀλλ᾽ ἀνταποδιδόασιν
ᾗ φανεροί εἰσι διὰ τὴν ὀξύτητα, εἶτ᾽ ἀποπαύονται.
ὑπερβολῇ δ᾽ εἰσὶν οἱ ἀκρόχολοι ὀξεῖς καὶ πρὸς πᾶν
ὀργίλοι καὶ ἐπὶ παντί· ὅθεν καὶ τοὔνομα.

οἱ δὲ πικροὶ δυσδιάλυτοι, καὶ πολὺν χρόνον ὀρ-
γίζονται· κατέχουσι γὰρ τὸν θυμόν. παῦλα δὲ γίνεται ὅταν ἀνταποδιδῷ· ἡ γὰρ τιμωρία παύει τῆς
ὀργῆς, ἡδονὴν ἀντὶ τῆς λύπης ἐμποιοῦσα. τούτου
δὲ μὴ γινομένου τὸ βάρος ἔχουσιν· διὰ γὰρ τὸ μὴ
ἐπιφανὲς εἶναι οὐδὲ συμπείθει αὐτοὺς οὐδείς, ἐν
αὑτῷ δὲ πέψαι τὴν ὀργὴν χρόνου δεῖ. εἰσὶ δ᾽ οἱ
τοιοῦτοι ἑαυτοῖς ὀχληρότατοι καὶ τοῖς μάλιστα
φίλοις.

χαλεποὺς δὲ λέγομεν τοὺς ἐφ᾽ οἷς τε μὴ δεῖ χαλεπαίνοντας καὶ μᾶλλον ἢ δεῖ καὶ πλείω χρόνον,
καὶ μὴ διαλλαττομένους ἄνευ τιμωρίας ἢ κολά-
σεως. τῇ πραότητι δὲ μᾶλλον τὴν ὑπερβολὴν ἀντι-
τίθεμεν· καὶ γὰρ μᾶλλον γίνεται· ἀνθρωπικώτερον

which is the best thing about them. This happens because their anger is so sharp that they don't hold it in; it is manifest when they lash out, but then it is over. Irritable people are exceedingly quick to anger—at everyone and about everything—hence their name.

Bitter people are hard to appease, and remain angry for a long time. That is because they hold in their temper. You stop being angry when you retaliate, since revenge puts an end to anger and replaces pain with pleasure. Bitter people, who don't retaliate, carry a heavy burden. Their anger isn't visible, no one talks them out of it, and it takes time to ripen inside them. These sorts of people are most burdensome to themselves and to their closest friends.

We call people harsh if they get angry about the wrong things, more strongly and for longer than they should, and they are not satisfied unless they exact vengeance or punishment. We are more likely to contrast *even temper* with the excess, since it is more widespread—it being

γὰρ τὸ τιμωρεῖσθαι· καὶ πρὸς τὸ συμβιοῦν οἱ χα-
λεποὶ χείρους. . . .

[4.6] Ἐν δὲ ταῖς ὁμιλίαις καὶ τῷ συζῆν καὶ λόγων
καὶ πραγμάτων κοινωνεῖν οἱ μὲν ἄρεσκοι δοκοῦσιν εἶναι, οἱ πάντα πρὸς ἡδονὴν ἐπαινοῦντες καὶ
οὐθὲν ἀντιτείνοντες, ἀλλ᾽ οἰόμενοι δεῖν ἄλυποι
τοῖς ἐντυγχάνουσιν εἶναι· οἱ δ᾽ ἐξ ἐναντίας τούτοις
πρὸς πάντα ἀντιτείνοντες καὶ τοῦ λυπεῖν οὐδ᾽
ὁτιοῦν φροντίζοντες δύσκολοι καὶ δυσέριδες
καλοῦνται. ὅτι μὲν οὖν αἱ εἰρημέναι ἕξεις ψε-
κταί εἰσιν, οὐκ ἄδηλον, καὶ ὅτι ἡ μέση τούτων

VIRTUE AND VICE IN ACTION

especially human to exact revenge—and harsh people are worse to live with. . . .

The next three chapters discuss a suite of virtues whose domain is social interactions. Chapter 6 focuses on the ways we can make others feel good, or bad, by the way we respond to them in social situations.

GETTING ALONG WITH OTHERS

[4.6] In the give-and-take of living with others, in what we say and do in company, some people seem *obsequious*. They praise everything you do or say, in order to be pleasant, and they oppose nothing. In their view, you must not be unpleasant to anyone you encounter. The opposite type oppose everything and don't care at all about making someone feel bad. We call that sort *disagreeable* and *contentious*. It is not hard to see that these two dispositions are blameworthy, and that the mean between them is praiseworthy.

ἐπαινετή, καθ' ἢν ἀποδέξεται ἃ δεῖ καὶ ὡς δεῖ,
ὁμοίως δὲ καὶ δυσχερανεῖ· ὄνομα δ' οὐκ ἀποδέδο-
ται αὐτῇ τι, ἔοικε δὲ μάλιστα φιλίᾳ. τοιοῦτος γάρ
ἐστιν ὁ κατὰ τὴν μέσην ἕξιν οἷον βουλόμεθα λέγειν τὸν ἐπιεικῆ φίλον, τὸ στέργειν προσλαβόν-
τα. διαφέρει δὲ τῆς φιλίας, ὅτι ἄνευ πάθους
ἐστὶ καὶ τοῦ στέργειν οἷς ὁμιλεῖ· οὐ γὰρ τῷ φιλεῖν
ἢ ἐχθαίρειν ἀποδέχεται ἕκαστα ὡς δεῖ, ἀλλὰ τῷ
τοιοῦτος εἶναι. . . .

καθόλου μὲν οὖν εἴρηται ὅτι ὡς δεῖ ὁμιλήσει,
ἀναφέρων δὲ πρὸς τὸ καλὸν καὶ τὸ συμφέρον
στοχάσεται τοῦ μὴ[1] λυπεῖν ἢ συνηδύνειν. ἔοικε
μὲν γὰρ περὶ ἡδονὰς καὶ λύπας εἶναι τὰς ἐν ταῖς
ὁμιλίαις γινομένας· τούτων δ' ὅσας μὲν αὐτῷ ἐστι
μὴ καλὸν ἢ βλαβερὸν συνηδύνειν, δυσχερανεῖ,
καὶ προαιρήσεται λυπεῖν· κἂν τῷ ποιοῦντι δ'

You strike the mean in give-and-take if you approve of or object to the right things and in the right way. There is no name for the intermediate disposition, but it is most like friendship,[20] since it makes you the sort of person we think of as a good friend (if affection is added to it). It differs from friendship in that you do not need to have a particular feeling or feel affection for the people you are dealing with. You will react in each case as you should, but not because you like or dislike the other person; it is because that is the sort of person you are. . . .

In general, as we said, you will engage in appropriate give-and-take with others. However, you will keep in mind what is decent and beneficial as you seek to be pleasant, or try not to be unpleasant. You are concerned with the pleasures and pains arising from give-and-take with others, but in situations where it would be indecent or harmful to be pleasant to the other person, you will choose to be unpleasant; you will object. Also, if what the other person proposes

ἀσχημοσύνην φέρῃ, καὶ ταύτην μὴ μικράν, ἢ βλά-
βην, ἡ δ᾽ ἐναντίωσις μικρὰν λύπην, οὐκ ἀποδέξεται ἀλλὰ δυσχερανεῖ.

διαφερόντως δ᾽ ὁμιλήσει τοῖς ἐν ἀξιώμασι καὶ
τοῖς τυχοῦσι, καὶ μᾶλλον ἢ ἧττον γνωρίμοις,
ὁμοίως δὲ καὶ κατὰ τὰς ἄλλας διαφοράς, ἑκάστοις
ἀπονέμων τὸ πρέπον, καὶ καθ᾽ αὑτὸ μὲν αἱρούμε-
νος τὸ συνηδύνειν, λυπεῖν δ᾽ εὐλαβούμενος, τοῖς
δ᾽ ἀποβαίνουσιν, ἐὰν ᾖ μείζω, συνεπόμενος, λέγω
δὲ τῷ καλῷ καὶ τῷ συμφέροντι. καὶ ἡδονῆς δ᾽
ἕνεκα τῆς εἰσαῦθις μεγάλης μικρὰ λυπήσει. ὁ μὲν
οὖν μέσος τοιοῦτός ἐστιν, οὐκ ὠνόμασται δέ·

τοῦ δὲ συνηδύνοντος ὁ μὲν τοῦ ἡδὺς εἶναι στο-
χαζόμενος μὴ διά τι ἄλλο ἄρεσκος, ὁ δ᾽ ὅπως
ὠφέλειά τις αὑτῷ γίνηται εἰς χρήματα καὶ ὅσα διὰ

to do would bring disgrace or harm upon them, and not in a small way, and if opposing it would cause them only slight pain, you will not go along with it; you will object.

You won't engage with dignitaries in the same way as with just anyone, or with people you know well in the same way as with people less familiar to you; but in line with these and other distinctions, you will treat each person appropriately, and will choose to be pleasant, or to avoid causing pain, for its own sake. But if the consequences of doing so are significant—in terms of whether it is decent or beneficial—you will heed those consequences. Also, you will cause a slight pain as the price for bringing about a large pleasure in return. That is what it is like to strike the mean, even though there is no name for it.

Now, people pleasers are *obsequious* if they aim at being pleasant, with no ulterior motive. But if their aim is to gain advantage for themselves, either in wealth or in what wealth can get

χρημάτων, κόλαξ· ὁ δὲ πᾶσι δυσχεραίνων εἴρηται
ὅτι δύσκολος καὶ δύσερις . . .

[4.8] Οὔσης δὲ καὶ ἀναπαύσεως ἐν τῷ βίῳ, καὶ ἐν
ταύτῃ διαγωγῆς μετὰ παιδιᾶς, δοκεῖ καὶ ἐνταῦθα
εἶναι ὁμιλία τις ἐμμελής, καὶ οἷα δεῖ λέγειν καὶ ὥς,
ὁμοίως δὲ καὶ ἀκούειν . . . οἱ μὲν οὖν τῷ γελοίῳ

them, they are *panderers*. As we have already stated, people who complain about everything are *disagreeable* and *contentious*. . . .

Chapter 7 discusses a very special kind of honesty—how you present yourself to others—not exaggerating your accomplishments or mentioning them unnecessarily, but not selling yourself short, either. Chapter 8 returns to the pleasures and pains of social interaction, this time in the context of telling, listening to, and being the butt of jokes.

Fun and Games

[4.8] Now life includes recreation, and that includes telling jokes. Here too, it seems, there is a right note to hit when engaging with others—what sort of jokes you should tell, how you should tell them, and how you should respond to the jokes that you hear. . . . People

ὑπερβάλλοντες βωμολόχοι δοκοῦσιν εἶναι καὶ
φορτικοί, γλιχόμενοι πάντως τοῦ γελοίου, καὶ
μᾶλλον στοχαζόμενοι τοῦ γέλωτα ποιῆσαι ἢ τοῦ
λέγειν εὐσχήμονα καὶ μὴ λυπεῖν τὸν σκωπτόμενον·
οἱ δὲ μήτ᾽ αὐτοὶ ἂν εἰπόντες μηδὲν γελοῖον τοῖς
τε λέγουσι δυσχεραίνοντες ἄγροικοι καὶ σκληροὶ
δοκοῦσιν εἶναι. οἱ δ᾽ ἐμμελῶς παίζοντες εὐτράπελοι προσαγορεύονται, οἷον εὔτροποι· τοῦ γὰρ
ἤθους αἱ τοιαῦται δοκοῦσι κινήσεις εἶναι, ὥσπερ
δὲ τὰ σώματα ἐκ τῶν κινήσεων κρίνεται, οὕτω
καὶ τὰ ἤθη. ἐπιπολάζοντος δὲ τοῦ γελοίου, καὶ τῶν
πλείστων χαιρόντων τῇ παιδιᾷ καὶ τῷ σκώπτειν
μᾶλλον ἢ δεῖ, καὶ οἱ βωμολόχοι εὐτράπελοι προσαγορεύονται ὡς χαρίεντες· ὅτι δὲ διαφέρουσι, καὶ
οὐ μικρόν, ἐκ τῶν εἰρημένων δῆλον.

τῇ μέσῃ δ᾽ ἕξει οἰκεῖον καὶ ἡ ἐπιδεξιότης ἐστίν·
τοῦ δ᾽ ἐπιδεξίου ἐστὶ τοιαῦτα λέγειν καὶ ἀκούειν

who go to excess in provoking laughter strike us as vulgar *buffoons*, always striving to be funny. Their aim is more to provoke laughter than to watch their language or to avoid causing pain to whoever is the butt of their joke. People who never say anything funny themselves, and object when other people do, seem to be *boorish* and stiff. When people's jokes are properly modulated, we say they have a *good sense of humor*, meaning their character is good. That is because the jokes people tell are like movements of their character, and just as we judge bodies from their motions, we do the same with character. Lots of things make us laugh, and most of us enjoy jokes and mockery more than we should, so even *buffoons* are credited with a sense of humor and considered witty. But it is clear from what we have said that there is a big difference between them.

The intermediate disposition involves deftness as well. A deft person will tell and will

οἷα τῷ ἐπιεικεῖ καὶ ἐλευθερίῳ ἁρμόττει· . . . οὐ δὴ
πᾶν ποιήσει· τὸ γὰρ σκῶμμα λοιδόρημά τι ἐστίν,
οἱ δὲ νομοθέται ἔνια λοιδορεῖν κωλύουσιν· ἔδει
δ' ἴσως καὶ σκώπτειν. ὁ δὴ χαρίεις καὶ ἐλευθέριος
οὕτως ἕξει, οἷον νόμος ὢν ἑαυτῷ. τοιοῦτος μὲν
οὖν ὁ μέσος ἐστίν, εἴτ' ἐπιδέξιος εἴτ' εὐτράπελος
λέγεται. ὁ δὲ βωμολόχος ἥττων ἐστὶ τοῦ γελοίου,
καὶ οὔτε ἑαυτοῦ οὔτε τῶν ἄλλων ἀπεχόμενος εἰ
γέλωτα ποιήσει, καὶ τοιαῦτα λέγων ὧν οὐδὲν ἂν
εἴποι ὁ χαρίεις, ἔνια δ' οὐδ' ἂν ἀκούσαι. ὁ δ'
ἄγροικος εἰς τὰς τοιαύτας ὁμιλίας ἀχρεῖος· οὐθὲν
γὰρ συμβαλλόμενος πᾶσι δυσχεραίνει. . . .

listen to the sorts of jokes that are fitting for a decent and well-bred person. . . . They won't tell just any joke. For example, a joke at someone else's expense is abusive, and legislators prohibit some forms of abuse; perhaps they should have prohibited this kind of joke as well. Indeed, that's the kind of disposition a witty and well-bred person will have; they are like a law for themselves. That's what the intermediate person is like, whether we call them *deft* or say they have a *good sense of humor*. A buffoon, by contrast, can't resist a joke and will raise a laugh even at their own expense, or at the expense of others. Buffoons will say things that a person of good taste would never say, and in some cases, would not even listen to. A boorish person is useless in such encounters, since they contribute nothing and object to everything. . . .

In the next chapter, which concludes book 4, Aristotle argues that shame is not a virtue.

[5.1] ... Ἐπεὶ δ' ὁ παράνομος ἄδικος ἦν ὁ δὲ νόμι-
μος δίκαιος, δῆλον ὅτι πάντα τὰ νόμιμά ἐστί πως
δίκαια· ... προστάττει δ' ὁ νόμος καὶ τὰ τοῦ ἀνδρείου ἔργα ποιεῖν, οἷον μὴ λείπειν τὴν τάξιν μηδὲ
φεύγειν μηδὲ ῥιπτεῖν τὰ ὅπλα, καὶ τὰ τοῦ σώφρονος, οἷον μὴ μοιχεύειν μηδ' ὑβρίζειν, καὶ τὰ τοῦ
πράου, οἷον μὴ τύπτειν μηδὲ κακηγορεῖν, ὁμοίως
δὲ καὶ κατὰ τὰς ἄλλας ἀρετὰς καὶ μοχθηρίας τὰ

JUSTICE

Aristotle devotes the entirety of book 5 to justice. In the most general sense, he states, justice is a matter of how we treat other people and thus overlaps with the virtues already discussed. In a more specific sense, justice has to do with the distribution of goods between persons, and the rectification of transgressions.

[5.1] . . . Since a lawbreaker is an unjust person, and someone who follows the law is a just person, there is clearly a way in which all lawful activity is just. . . . But the law also commands acts of bravery, such as not breaking ranks, fleeing, or throwing away your armor. It commands acts of self-discipline as well (since it forbids adultery and rape) and even-tempered acts (since it forbids us to hit people or mistreat them), and likewise for the other virtues and vices. The law urges us toward some acts and away from others—correctly when the law is

μὲν κελεύων τὰ δ᾽ ἀπαγορεύων, ὀρθῶς μὲν ὁ κείμενος ὀρθῶς, χεῖρον δ᾽ ὁ ἀπεσχεδιασμένος.

αὕτη μὲν οὖν ἡ δικαιοσύνη ἀρετὴ μέν ἐστι τελεία, ἀλλ᾽ οὐχ ἁπλῶς ἀλλὰ πρὸς ἕτερον. καὶ διὰ τοῦτο πολλάκις κρατίστη τῶν ἀρετῶν εἶναι δοκεῖ ἡ δικαιοσύνη, . . . διὰ δὲ τὸ αὐτὸ τοῦτο καὶ ἀλλότριον ἀγαθὸν δοκεῖ εἶναι ἡ δικαιοσύνη μόνη τῶν ἀρετῶν, ὅτι πρὸς ἕτερόν ἐστιν· ἄλλῳ γὰρ τὰ συμφέροντα πράττει, ἢ ἄρχοντι ἢ κοινωνῷ. . . . αὕτη μὲν οὖν ἡ δικαιοσύνη οὐ μέρος ἀρετῆς ἀλλ᾽ ὅλη ἀρετή ἐστιν, οὐδ᾽ ἡ ἐναντία ἀδικία μέρος κακίας ἀλλ᾽ ὅλη κακία. . . .

[5.2] . . . τῆς δὲ κατὰ μέρος δικαιοσύνης καὶ τοῦ κατ᾽ αὐτὴν δικαίου ἓν μέν ἐστιν εἶδος τὸ ἐν ταῖς διανομαῖς τιμῆς ἢ χρημάτων ἢ τῶν ἄλλων ὅσα μεριστὰ τοῖς κοινωνοῦσι τῆς πολιτείας (ἐν τούτοις γὰρ ἔστι καὶ ἄνισον ἔχειν καὶ ἴσον ἕτερον ἑτέρου), ἓν δὲ τὸ ἐν τοῖς συναλλάγμασι διορθωτικόν.

made correctly, and badly when the law is poorly drafted.

This kind of justice encompasses virtue completely, but with a qualification; it is virtue in relation to another person. That is why justice often seems to be the most important of the virtues. . . . And it is also why justice is the only virtue that seems to be another person's good . . . (a just person does what is good for another, whether that is the ruler or a fellow citizen). . . . So, this kind of justice is not a part of virtue; it is the whole of virtue. And the opposite, injustice, is not a part of vice; it is vice in its entirety. . . .

[5.2] . . . As for the justice that is *a part* of virtue, and the corresponding way of being just, one kind has to do with the distribution of honor or wealth or other goods that are divisible among a city's citizens. (With these goods it is possible for what one person has to be fair or unfair in relation to what another person has.) Another kind has to do with rectifying

τούτου δὲ μέρη δύο· τῶν γὰρ συναλλαγμάτων τὰ μὲν ἑκούσιά ἐστι τὰ δ' ἀκούσια, ἑκούσια μὲν τὰ τοιάδε οἷον πρᾶσις ὠνὴ δανεισμὸς ἐγγύη χρῆσις παρακαταθήκη μίσθωσις (ἑκούσια δὲ λέγεται, ὅτι ἡ ἀρχὴ τῶν συναλλαγμάτων τούτων ἑκούσιος), τῶν δ' ἀκουσίων τὰ μὲν λαθραῖα, οἷον κλοπὴ μοιχεία φαρμακεία προαγωγεία δουλαπατία δολοφονία ψευδομαρτυρία, τὰ δὲ βίαια, οἷον αἰκία δεσμὸς θάνατος ἁρπαγὴ πήρωσις κακηγορία προπηλακισμός.

interactions between people. It has two parts, since some interactions are voluntary and others are involuntary. Voluntary interactions include such things as selling, buying, lending, pledging security, hiring, entrusting deposits, and leasing out. (We call these transactions voluntary because their origin is voluntary.) Involuntary interactions can be by stealth, as in the case of theft, adultery, poisoning, procuring, enticement, deadly treachery, or perjury. Or they can be by force—for example: assaulting someone, throwing them in chains, putting them to death, or robbing, maiming, slandering, or insulting them.

The remaining chapters of book 5 discuss the details of distributive and rectificatory justice and propose that justice is a mean between committing injustice and being unjustly treated. Aristotle also addresses some puzzles (taken over from Plato) about whether you can commit injustice involuntarily.

[6.1] Ἐπεὶ δὲ τυγχάνομεν πρότερον εἰρηκότες ὅτι δεῖ τὸ μέσον αἱρεῖσθαι, μὴ τὴν ὑπερβολὴν μηδὲ τὴν ἔλλειψιν, τὸ δὲ μέσον ἐστὶν ὡς ὁ λόγος ὁ ὀρθὸς λέγει, τοῦτο διέλωμεν. ἐν πάσαις γὰρ ταῖς εἰρημέναις ἕξεσι, καθάπερ καὶ ἐπὶ τῶν ἄλλων, ἔστι τις σκοπὸς πρὸς ὃν ἀποβλέπων ὁ τὸν λόγον ἔχων ἐπιτείνει καὶ ἀνίησιν, καί τις ἔστιν ὅρος τῶν μεσοτήτων, ἃς μεταξύ φαμεν εἶναι τῆς ὑπερβολῆς καὶ τῆς ἐλλείψεως, οὔσας κατὰ τὸν ὀρθὸν λόγον. ἔστι δὲ τὸ μὲν εἰπεῖν οὕτως ἀληθὲς μέν, οὐθὲν δὲ σαφές· καὶ γὰρ ἐν ταῖς ἄλλαις ἐπιμελείαις, περὶ

5. VIRTUES FOR A THINKING PERSON

(Book 6)

Uses of the Mind

[6.1] We previously stated that a person should avoid excess and deficiency and select the mean, and that the mean is what correct thinking dictates. Now let us define what that involves. In all the dispositions we have listed, just as in other cases, there is a target that a thinking person keeps in view when adjusting their aim, something that demarcates the intermediate dispositions. We say the intermediate dispositions are between excess and deficiency, and follow correct thinking. But while that statement is true, it is not particularly clear. We could say the same thing about expert care in any other

ὅσας ἐστὶν ἐπιστήμη, τοῦτ' ἀληθὲς μὲν εἰπεῖν, ὅτι οὔτε πλείω οὔτε ἐλάττω δεῖ πονεῖν οὐδὲ ῥαθυμεῖν, ἀλλὰ τὰ μέσα καὶ ὡς ὁ ὀρθὸς λόγος· τοῦτο δὲ μόνον ἔχων ἄν τις οὐδὲν ἂν εἰδείη πλέον, οἷον ποῖα δεῖ προσφέρεσθαι πρὸς τὸ σῶμα, εἴ τις εἴπειεν ὅτι ὅσα ἡ ἰατρικὴ κελεύει καὶ ὡς ὁ ταύτην ἔχων. διὸ δεῖ καὶ περὶ τὰς τῆς ψυχῆς ἕξεις μὴ μόνον ἀληθῶς εἶναι τοῦτ' εἰρημένον, ἀλλὰ καὶ διωρισμένον τίς ἐστιν ὁ ὀρθὸς λόγος καὶ τούτου τίς ὅρος.

Τὰς δὴ τῆς ψυχῆς ἀρετὰς διελόμενοι τὰς μὲν εἶναι τοῦ ἤθους ἔφαμεν τὰς δὲ τῆς διανοίας. περὶ μὲν οὖν τῶν ἠθικῶν διεληλύθαμεν, περὶ δὲ τῶν λοιπῶν, περὶ ψυχῆς πρῶτον εἰπόντες, λέγωμεν οὕτως. πρότερον μὲν οὖν ἐλέχθη δύ' εἶναι μέρη τῆς ψυχῆς, τό τε λόγον ἔχον καὶ τὸ ἄλογον· νῦν δὲ περὶ τοῦ λόγον ἔχοντος τὸν αὐτὸν τρόπον διαιρετέον. καὶ ὑποκείσθω δύο τὰ λόγον ἔχοντα, ἓν μὲν ᾧ θεωροῦμεν τὰ τοιαῦτα τῶν ὄντων ὅσων αἱ

domain: that you should not engage in an activity—or hold back from it—too much nor too little; your actions should strike the mean and follow correct thinking. However, we would be no wiser about what sorts of remedies to apply to a body if the only information we had was that you should do *what medicine dictates* and *what a medical expert would do*. So we need more than this truism about the dispositions of the soul. We need to be more specific about what correct thinking is and what defines it.

When we distinguished the different virtues of the soul, we called some of them virtues of character and others virtues of intellect. Since we have dealt with the virtues of character, let us now discuss the other kind—beginning with some remarks about the soul. In our earlier discussion we said the soul has two parts, a thinking part and a part that is unthinking. Now we must likewise divide the thinking part. Let us stipulate that there are two thinking parts. With one of them we consider things whose

ἀρχαὶ μὴ ἐνδέχονται ἄλλως ἔχειν, ἓν δὲ ᾧ τὰ ἐν-
δεχόμενα· . . . λεγέσθω δὲ τούτων τὸ μὲν ἐπιστη-
μονικὸν τὸ δὲ λογιστικόν· τὸ γὰρ βουλεύεσθαι
καὶ λογίζεσθαι ταὐτόν, οὐδεὶς δὲ βουλεύεται περὶ
τῶν μὴ ἐνδεχομένων ἄλλως ἔχειν. ὥστε τὸ λογι-
στικόν ἐστιν ἕν τι μέρος τοῦ λόγον ἔχοντος.

ληπτέον ἄρ' ἑκατέρου τούτων τίς ἡ βελτίστη
ἕξις· αὕτη γὰρ ἀρετὴ ἑκατέρου, ἡ δ' ἀρετὴ πρὸς
τὸ ἔργον τὸ οἰκεῖον.

principles cannot be otherwise; with the other we consider things that can be otherwise.... Let us call these the *scientific* part and the *reasoning* part (since deliberating is the same as reasoning and no one deliberates about things that cannot be otherwise). The *reasoning* part is therefore one component of the thinking part of our souls.

We need to identify the best disposition of each of these parts. That will be its virtue and will involve the activity that properly belongs to it.

Aristotle above registers a significant disagreement with Plato, for whom the entire thinking part of the soul is the "reasoning part."[21] Aristotle insists that there are two very different types of thinking. He will occasionally call the activity of the SCIENTIFIC *part of the soul "theoretical" thinking, and the activity of the* REASONING *part "action-oriented" or "productive" thinking.[22]*

[6.2] . . . τῆς δὲ θεωρητικῆς διανοίας καὶ μὴ πρα-
κτικῆς μηδὲ ποιητικῆς τὸ εὖ καὶ κακῶς τἀληθές
ἐστι καὶ ψεῦδος (τοῦτο γάρ ἐστι παντὸς διανοητικοῦ ἔργον)· τοῦ δὲ πρακτικοῦ καὶ διανοητικοῦ
ἀλήθεια ὁμολόγως ἔχουσα τῇ ὀρέξει τῇ ὀρθῇ.
πράξεως μὲν οὖν ἀρχὴ προαίρεσις—ὅθεν ἡ κίνη-
σις ἀλλ᾽ οὐχ οὗ ἕνεκα—προαιρέσεως δὲ ὄρεξις
καὶ λόγος ὁ ἕνεκά τινος . . . διὸ ἢ ὀρεκτικὸς νοῦς
ἡ προαίρεσις ἢ ὄρεξις διανοητική . . .

ἀμφοτέρων δὴ τῶν νοητικῶν μορίων ἀλήθεια
τὸ ἔργον. καθ᾽ ἃς οὖν μάλιστα ἕξεις ἀληθεύσει
ἑκάτερον, αὗται ἀρεταὶ ἀμφοῖν.

[6.3] . . . ἔστω δὴ οἷς ἀληθεύει ἡ ψυχὴ τῷ κατα-
φάναι ἢ ἀποφάναι, πέντε τὸν ἀριθμόν· ταῦτα δ᾽

[6.2] ... When we engage in *theoretical* thinking (rather than action-oriented or productive thinking), we are doing it well or badly according to whether our thoughts are true or false — since that is what any thinking part does. When we engage in *action-oriented* thinking, we are doing it well when what we think is true *and* it agrees with correct desire. That's because action originates in choice, and choice arises from desire plus goal-directed thinking ... (which makes choice either desiderative thought, or desire informed by thought). ...

Since grasping truth is an activity belonging to both intellectual parts, the virtues of those parts will be whatever dispositions make them especially good at grasping the truth.

Virtues of the Mind

[6.3] ... Let us distinguish five dispositions by which the soul grasps the truth in its affirmations and denials. These are *art, scientific knowledge,*

ἐστὶ τέχνη ἐπιστήμη φρόνησις σοφία νοῦς· ὑπο-
λήψει γὰρ καὶ δόξῃ ἐνδέχεται διαψεύδεσθαι.

ἐπιστήμη μὲν οὖν τί ἐστιν, ἐντεῦθεν φανερόν, εἰ
δεῖ ἀκριβολογεῖσθαι καὶ μὴ ἀκολουθεῖν ταῖς
ὁμοιότησιν. πάντες γὰρ ὑπολαμβάνομεν, ὃ ἐπι-
στάμεθα, μηδ᾽ ἐνδέχεσθαι ἄλλως ἔχειν· . . . . ἐξ
ἀνάγκης ἄρα ἐστὶ τὸ ἐπιστητόν. ἀίδιον ἄρα· τὰ
γὰρ ἐξ ἀνάγκης ὄντα ἁπλῶς πάντα ἀίδια, τὰ δ᾽
ἀίδια ἀγένητα καὶ ἄφθαρτα.

good judgment, *scientific learning*, and *scientific apprehension*. (Supposition and belief, on the other hand, can be false.)

The names Aristotle assigns above to these five intellectual virtues are ordinary Greek words for knowledge, but he is using them in narrow, technical senses. The English translations line up roughly with his stipulated definitions, rather than with their ordinary meanings.

Scientific Knowledge

If we want to make precise distinctions, and not get drawn in by similarities, here is how we clarify *scientific knowledge*. We all suppose that things we *know scientifically* are not even capable of being otherwise. . . . So the objects of science are necessary, and also eternal—since what is necessary is plainly eternal and what is eternal neither comes to be nor passes away.

ἔτι διδακτὴ ἄπασα ἐπιστήμη δοκεῖ εἶναι, καὶ τὸ ἐπιστητὸν μαθητόν. ἐκ προγινωσκομένων δὲ πᾶσα διδασκαλία, ὥσπερ καὶ ἐν τοῖς ἀναλυτικοῖς λέγομεν· ἢ μὲν γὰρ δι᾽ ἐπαγωγῆς, ἢ δὲ συλλογισμῷ. ἡ μὲν δὴ ἐπαγωγὴ ἀρχή ἐστι καὶ τοῦ καθόλου, ὁ δὲ συλλογισμὸς ἐκ τῶν καθόλου. εἰσὶν ἄρα ἀρχαὶ ἐξ ὧν ὁ συλλογισμός, ὧν οὐκ ἔστι συλλογισμός· ἐπαγωγὴ ἄρα. ἡ μὲν ἄρα ἐπιστήμη ἐστὶν ἕξις ἀποδεικτική, καὶ ὅσα ἄλλα προσδιοριζόμεθα ἐν τοῖς ἀναλυτικοῖς· ὅταν γάρ πως πιστεύῃ καὶ γνώριμοι αὐτῷ ὦσιν αἱ ἀρχαί, ἐπίσταται· . . . περὶ μὲν οὖν ἐπιστήμης διωρίσθω τὸν τρόπον τοῦτον.

Furthermore, every science seems to be teachable, and its objects can be learned. As we explain in the *Analytics*, all teaching draws on prior knowledge. Some, for example, proceeds by induction, which leads us *to* the universal, and other teaching proceeds by deduction, which proceeds *from* the universal. (Some principles of deduction have no deduction; they must be learned by induction.) So *scientific knowledge* is a disposition for demonstration[23] and has the other features we discuss in the *Analytics*. When you have been persuaded in a way, and are familiar with the principles, you have scientific knowledge. . . . Let this be how we demarcate *scientific knowledge*.

Aristotle elaborates this very narrow conception of science in the POSTERIOR ANALYTICS, *where he explains that we have scientific knowledge only of necessary truths demonstrated from first principles.*

[6.4] Τοῦ δ᾽ ἐνδεχομένου ἄλλως ἔχειν ἔστι τι καὶ ποιητὸν καὶ πρακτόν· ἕτερον δ᾽ ἐστὶ ποίησις καὶ πρᾶξις . . .

ἐπεὶ δ᾽ ἡ οἰκοδομικὴ τέχνη τίς ἐστι καὶ ὅπερ ἕξις τις μετὰ λόγου ποιητική, καὶ οὐδεμία οὔτε τέχνη ἐστὶν ἥτις οὐ μετὰ λόγου ποιητικὴ ἕξις ἐστίν, οὔτε τοιαύτη ἢ οὐ τέχνη, ταὐτὸν ἂν εἴη τέχνη καὶ ἕξις μετὰ λόγου ἀληθοῦς ποιητική. ἔστι δὲ τέχνη πᾶσα περὶ γένεσιν καὶ τὸ τεχνάζειν καὶ θεωρεῖν ὅπως ἂν γένηταί τι τῶν ἐνδεχομένων καὶ εἶναι καὶ μὴ εἶναι, καὶ ὧν ἡ ἀρχὴ ἐν τῷ ποιοῦντι ἀλλὰ μὴ ἐν τῷ ποιουμένῳ· οὔτε γὰρ τῶν ἐξ ἀνάγκης ὄντων ἢ γινομένων ἡ τέχνη ἐστίν, οὔτε τῶν κατὰ φύσιν· ἐν αὑτοῖς γὰρ ἔχουσι ταῦτα τὴν ἀρχήν. . . .

ἡ μὲν οὖν τέχνη, ὥσπερ εἴρηται, ἕξις τις μετὰ λόγου ἀληθοῦς ποιητική ἐστιν, ἡ δ᾽ ἀτεχνία

Art

[6.4] What is capable of being otherwise in-cludes products that can be made and actions that can be performed. And production is dif-ferent from action. . . .

Since house building is an *art*, and is in effect a disposition for production based on thinking, and there is no art that is not such a disposition — and no such disposition that is not an art — an *art* would be the same thing as a disposition for production based on true thinking. Every kind of *art* is about coming into being. It figures out and devises means to bring about something that is capable both of being and of not being, something that originates in the maker, not in the thing made. There is no *art* for producing things whose existence or occurrence is neces-sary, or for producing natural things, since these have their origin in themselves.[24] . . .

So, as we said, an *art* is a disposition for production based on true thinking, while the

τοὐναντίον μετὰ λόγου ψευδοῦς ποιητικὴ ἕξις, περὶ τὸ ἐνδεχόμενον ἄλλως ἔχειν.

[6.5] Περὶ δὲ φρονήσεως οὕτως ἂν λάβοιμεν, θεωρήσαντες τίνας λέγομεν τοὺς φρονίμους. δοκεῖ δὴ φρονίμου εἶναι τὸ δύνασθαι καλῶς βουλεύσασθαι περὶ τὰ αὑτῷ ἀγαθὰ καὶ συμφέροντα, οὐ κατὰ μέρος, οἷον ποῖα πρὸς ὑγίειαν, πρὸς ἰσχύν, ἀλλὰ ποῖα πρὸς τὸ εὖ ζῆν ὅλως . . . ὥστε καὶ ὅλως ἂν εἴη φρόνιμος ὁ βουλευτικός. βουλεύεται δ᾽ οὐθεὶς περὶ τῶν ἀδυνάτων ἄλλως ἔχειν, οὐδὲ τῶν μὴ ἐνδεχομένων αὑτῷ πρᾶξαι. ὥστ᾽ . . . οὐκ ἂν εἴη ἡ φρόνησις ἐπιστήμη οὐδὲ τέχνη, ἐπιστήμη μὲν

opposite condition, in the amateur, is a disposition for production based on mistaken thinking. The objects of this knowledge are capable of being otherwise.

Aristotle's other examples of arts include shipbuilding and medicine, as well as skill at writing or playing a musical instrument.

Good Judgment

[6.5] We might grasp what *good judgment* is by considering those to whom we ascribe it. People with *good judgment*, it seems, are capable of excellent deliberation about what is good for them and useful—not with a view to some particular objective such as health or strength, but more generally with a view to living well. . . . So, in general, people who are good at deliberating have *good judgment*. Now, no one deliberates about what cannot be otherwise or what isn't something they themselves can do, so . . . *good judgment* would be distinct from *scientific*

ὅτι ἐνδέχεται τὸ πρακτὸν ἄλλως ἔχειν, τέχνη δ᾽ ὅτι ἄλλο τὸ γένος πράξεως καὶ ποιήσεως. λείπεται ἄρα αὐτὴν εἶναι ἕξιν ἀληθῆ μετὰ λόγου πρακτικὴν περὶ τὰ ἀνθρώπῳ ἀγαθὰ καὶ κακά. τῆς μὲν γὰρ ποιήσεως ἕτερον τὸ τέλος, τῆς δὲ πράξεως οὐκ ἂν εἴη· ἔστι γὰρ αὐτὴ ἡ εὐπραξία τέλος.

διὰ τοῦτο Περικλέα καὶ τοὺς τοιούτους φρονίμους οἰόμεθα εἶναι, ὅτι τὰ αὑτοῖς ἀγαθὰ καὶ τὰ τοῖς ἀνθρώποις δύνανται θεωρεῖν· εἶναι δὲ τοιούτους ἡγούμεθα τοὺς οἰκονομικοὺς καὶ τοὺς πολιτικούς. ἔνθεν καὶ τὴν σωφροσύνην τούτῳ προσαγορεύομεν τῷ ὀνόματι, ὡς σῴζουσαν τὴν φρόνησιν. σῴζει δὲ τὴν τοιαύτην ὑπόληψιν. οὐ γὰρ ἅπασαν ὑπόληψιν διαφθείρει οὐδὲ διαστρέφει τὸ ἡδὺ καὶ λυπηρόν, οἷον ὅτι τὸ τρίγωνον δύο ὀρθὰς ἔχει ἢ οὐκ ἔχει, ἀλλὰ τὰς περὶ τὸ πρακτόν. αἱ μὲν γὰρ ἀρχαὶ τῶν πρακτῶν τὸ οὗ ἕνεκα τὰ

knowledge (since actions admit of being otherwise) and also from *art* (since production and action are different kinds of things). The remaining possibility is that it is a disposition to act based on true thinking about what is good and bad for a human being. (Production has a further goal, but action does not, since doing well itself is the goal of action.)

That is why we ascribe *good judgment* to Pericles[25] and people like him: they are good at grasping what is good for themselves and for human beings in general. (People good at managing household affairs and public affairs are like that, we think.) It is also why our term for self-discipline [*sōphrosunē*] indicates that it "preserves [*sōzein*] our good judgment [*phronēsis*]." It is precisely this sort of belief that self-discipline preserves. Not just any belief is destroyed or distorted by pleasure and pain—for example, not beliefs about whether the sum of a triangle's angles equals two right angles—only our beliefs about what to do. The principles of

πρακτά· τῷ δὲ διεφθαρμένῳ δι' ἡδονὴν ἢ λύπην
εὐθὺς οὐ φαίνεται ἀρχή, οὐδὲ δεῖν τούτου ἕνεκεν
οὐδὲ διὰ τοῦθ' αἱρεῖσθαι πάντα καὶ πράττειν· ἔστι
γὰρ ἡ κακία φθαρτικὴ ἀρχῆς.

ὥστ' ἀνάγκη τὴν φρόνησιν ἕξιν εἶναι μετὰ
λόγου ἀληθοῦς² περὶ τὰ ἀνθρώπινα ἀγαθὰ πρα-
κτικήν. . . . δυοῖν δ' ὄντοιν μεροῖν τῆς ψυχῆς τῶν
λόγον ἐχόντων, θατέρου ἂν εἴη ἀρετή, τοῦ δοξα-
στικοῦ· ἥ τε γὰρ δόξα περὶ τὸ ἐνδεχόμενον ἄλλως
ἔχειν καὶ ἡ φρόνησις. ἀλλὰ μὴν οὐδ' ἕξις μετὰ
λόγου μόνον· σημεῖον δ' ὅτι λήθη μὲν τῆς τοιαύτης
ἕξεως ἔστι, φρονήσεως δ' οὐκ ἔστιν.

our actions are the goals we aim at in acting, and someone who is corrupted by pleasure or pain does not see straightaway what the goal of their action should be, or that their choices and actions should all be directed toward it. Vice, you see, destroys the principle.

It follows that *good judgment* is a disposition to act based on true thinking about human goods. . . . Of the soul's two thinking parts, this virtue belongs to the part that forms beliefs (since belief is about things that admit of being otherwise, and the same is true for *good judgment*). And it is not simply a disposition based on thought—as shown by the fact that such a disposition can be forgotten, while *good judgment* cannot.

The next two chapters define two more virtues of the soul's "scientific" part. SCIENTIFIC APPREHENSION *(chapter 6) is knowledge of the first principles from which scientific knowledge is deduced.* SCIENTIFIC LEARNING *(chapter 7) is a*

[6.7] ... δῆλον ὅτι ἀκριβεστάτη ἂν τῶν ἐπιστημῶν εἴη ἡ σοφία. δεῖ ἄρα τὸν σοφὸν μὴ μόνον τὰ
ἐκ τῶν ἀρχῶν εἰδέναι, ἀλλὰ καὶ περὶ τὰς ἀρχὰς
ἀληθεύειν. ὥστ᾽ εἴη ἂν ἡ σοφία νοῦς καὶ ἐπιστήμη,
ὥσπερ κεφαλὴν ἔχουσα ἐπιστήμη τῶν τιμιω-
τάτων. ἄτοπον γὰρ εἴ τις τὴν πολιτικὴν ἢ τὴν

supreme intellectual accomplishment that involves having both scientific apprehension and scientific knowledge.

Scientific Learning

The translations "learning" and "learned" are used in the old-fashioned sense that refers to knowledge acquired from study, not the process of learning. The Greek term Aristotle uses is SOPHIA, *which has an ordinary meaning of "wisdom" or "knowledge," but he uses it here in a restricted technical sense.*

[6.7] . . . Clearly, *scientific learning* would be the most rigorous form of knowledge, since having such learning involves not only knowing what follows from the principles of a science, but also apprehending the truth of the principles themselves. So *scientific learning* would be *scientific apprehension* together with *scientific knowledge*—capstone knowledge, as it were, of the most venerable objects. After all, it would be strange to think that the art of politics, or

φρόνησιν σπουδαιοτάτην οἴεται εἶναι, εἰ μὴ τὸ
ἄριστον τῶν ἐν τῷ κόσμῳ ἄνθρωπός ἐστιν. . . .

εἰ δ᾽ ὅτι βέλτιστον ἄνθρωπος τῶν ἄλλων ζῴων,
οὐδὲν διαφέρει· καὶ γὰρ ἀνθρώπου ἄλλα πολὺ
θειότερα τὴν φύσιν, οἷον φανερώτατά γε ἐξ ὧν ὁ
κόσμος συνέστηκεν. ἐκ δὴ τῶν εἰρημένων δῆλον
ὅτι ἡ σοφία ἐστὶ καὶ ἐπιστήμη καὶ νοῦς τῶν τιμι-
ωτάτων τῇ φύσει.

διὸ Ἀναξαγόραν καὶ Θαλῆν καὶ τοὺς τοιούτους
σοφοὺς μὲν φρονίμους δ᾽ οὔ φασιν εἶναι, ὅταν
ἴδωσιν ἀγνοοῦντας τὰ συμφέροντα ἑαυτοῖς, καὶ
περιττὰ μὲν καὶ θαυμαστὰ καὶ χαλεπὰ καὶ δαι-
μόνια εἰδέναι αὐτούς φασιν, ἄχρηστα δ᾽, ὅτι οὐ τὰ
ἀνθρώπινα ἀγαθὰ ζητοῦσιν. Ἡ δὲ φρόνησις περὶ
τὰ ἀνθρώπινα καὶ περὶ ὧν ἔστι βουλεύσασθαι· τοῦ

good judgment, is the most excellent form of knowledge if a human being is not the greatest thing that exists in the cosmos. . . .

It makes no difference that a human being is the best of all the animals, for there are other things with a nature far more divine than a human being—the elements of the cosmos being the most obvious examples. So it is clear from what we have said that *scientific learning* is *scientific knowledge* combined with *scientific apprehension* of objects that are by nature the most venerable.

That is why people like Anaximander and Thales are said to have *scientific learning* but lack *good judgment*—when it seems they are ignorant about their own interests.[26] They are credited with knowing things that are extreme and amazing and difficult and divine—but useless—since they do not inquire into human goods. *Good judgment*, by contrast, is about human concerns. These are matters about which it is possible to deliberate, and deliberating well,

γὰρ φρονίμου μάλιστα τοῦτ᾽ ἔργον εἶναί φαμεν,
τὸ εὖ βουλεύεσθαι . . .

[6.8] Ἔστι δὲ καὶ ἡ πολιτικὴ καὶ ἡ φρόνησις ἡ
αὐτὴ μὲν ἕξις, τὸ μέντοι εἶναι οὐ ταὐτὸν αὐταῖς.
τῆς δὲ περὶ πόλιν ἣ μὲν ὡς ἀρχιτεκτονικὴ φρόνησις νομοθετική, ἣ δὲ ὡς τὰ καθ᾽ ἕκαστα τὸ κοινὸν
ἔχει ὄνομα, πολιτική· αὕτη δὲ πρακτικὴ καὶ βου-
λευτική· τὸ γὰρ ψήφισμα πρακτὸν ὡς τὸ ἔσχατον.
διὸ πολιτεύεσθαι τούτους μόνον λέγουσιν· μόνοι
γὰρ πράττουσιν οὗτοι ὥσπερ οἱ χειροτέχναι. δοκεῖ

we noted, belongs especially to the person of *good judgment. . . .*

In chapters 8 and 9 Aristotle considers two competences that are closely connected to good judgment: the ART OF POLITICS *(good judgment on a civic scale), and* GOOD DELIBERATION *(a component of good judgment).*

THE ART OF POLITICS

[6.8] Now the *art of politics* is the same disposition as *good judgment*, but differently defined. *Good judgment* about civic affairs in its most architectonic form is the *art of legislation. Good judgment* about particular courses of action for the city to take gets called the *art of politics* (even though that label belongs to both). The latter is action oriented and deliberative (since decrees are ultimately about action). Hence only in that domain are people described as practicing *politics* — since only they are actually doing

δὲ καὶ φρόνησις μάλιστ' εἶναι ἡ περὶ αὐτὸν καὶ
ἕνα· καὶ ἔχει αὕτη τὸ κοινὸν ὄνομα, φρόνησις·
ἐκείνων δὲ ἡ μὲν οἰκονομία ἡ δὲ νομοθεσία ἡ δὲ
πολιτική . . .

τοῦ γὰρ ἐσχάτου ἐστίν, ὥσπερ εἴρηται· τὸ γὰρ
πρακτὸν τοιοῦτον. ἀντίκειται μὲν δὴ τῷ νῷ· ὁ
μὲν γὰρ νοῦς τῶν ὅρων, ὧν οὐκ ἔστι λόγος, ἡ δὲ
τοῦ ἐσχάτου, οὗ οὐκ ἔστιν ἐπιστήμη ἀλλ'
αἴσθησις . . .

[6.9] . . . τὸ γὰρ βουλεύεσθαι ζητεῖν τι ἐστίν. δεῖ
δὲ λαβεῖν καὶ περὶ εὐβουλίας τί ἐστι . . . ἐπεὶ ὁ μὲν

things, like craftsmen plying their trade. *Good judgment* too strikes us as especially concerned with the individual — with your own situation — and *that* is what gets labeled with the generic name *good judgment*. But the various forms of *good judgment* include not only management of your own affairs, but also legislation, and the art of politics. . . .

Good judgment, like action, is concerned with ultimate particulars, as we said. So it is the diametrical opposite to *scientific apprehension*, because you *apprehend* ultimate definitions (for which no reason can be given) while you exercise *good judgment* about ultimate particulars. There is no *scientific knowledge* of these; you perceive them. . . .

GOOD DELIBERATION

[6.9] . . . Deliberation is a kind of inquiry, and *good deliberation* is something else we should grasp. What is it? . . . Since people who deliberate

κακῶς βουλευόμενος ἁμαρτάνει, ὁ δ᾽ εὖ ὀρθῶς βουλεύεται, δῆλον ὅτι ὀρθότης τις ἡ εὐβουλία ἐστίν. . . .

ἐπεὶ δ᾽ ἡ ὀρθότης πλεοναχῶς, δῆλον ὅτι οὐ πᾶσα· ὁ γὰρ ἀκρατὴς καὶ ὁ φαῦλος ὃ προτίθεται †ἰδεῖν† ἐκ τοῦ λογισμοῦ τεύξεται, ὥστε ὀρθῶς ἔσται βεβουλευμένος, κακὸν δὲ μέγα εἰληφώς. δοκεῖ δ᾽ ἀγαθόν τι τὸ εὖ βεβουλεῦσθαι· ἡ γὰρ τοιαύτη ὀρθότης βουλῆς εὐβουλία, ἡ ἀγαθοῦ τευ-κτική. ἀλλ᾽ ἔστι καὶ τούτου ψευδεῖ συλλογισμῷ τυχεῖν, καὶ ὃ μὲν δεῖ ποιῆσαι τυχεῖν, δι᾽ οὗ δ᾽ οὔ, . . . ὥστ᾽ οὐδ᾽ αὕτη πω εὐβουλία, . . . ἔτι ἔστι πολὺν χρόνον βουλευόμενον τυχεῖν, τὸν δὲ ταχύ. οὐκοῦν οὐδ᾽ ἐκείνη πω εὐβουλία, ἀλλ᾽ ὀρθότης ἡ κατὰ τὸ ὠφέλιμον, καὶ οὗ δεῖ καὶ ὡς καὶ ὅτε.

badly are mistaken, while those who deliberate well do so correctly, *good deliberation* is clearly a kind of correctness. . . .

Not every form of correctness in deliberation will be *good deliberation*. For example, if you lack self-control or are a bad person, you can still figure out how to accomplish your objective. You will have deliberated correctly, but secured a great evil. Deliberating well, however, is evidently something good; the deliberative correctness that is *good deliberation* is the sort that achieves good. However, it is possible to do so by faulty inference, and arrive at the right thing to do but through the wrong steps . . . so that that won't count as *good deliberation* either. . . . Also, it is possible to hit upon the right conclusion after taking a long time to deliberate, or to hit upon it quickly. The former does not count as *good deliberation*, which must be correct in having a beneficial result, arrived at through the right steps, in the right way, and at the right time.

ἔτι ἔστι καὶ ἁπλῶς εὖ βεβουλεῦσθαι καὶ πρός τι τέλος. ἢ μὲν δὴ ἁπλῶς ἡ πρὸς τὸ τέλος τὸ ἁπλῶς κατορθυῦσα, τὶς δὲ ἡ πρός τι τέλος. εἰ δὴ τῶν φρονίμων τὸ εὖ βεβουλεῦσθαι, ἡ εὐβουλία εἴη ἂν ὀρθότης ἡ κατὰ τὸ συμφέρον πρὸς τὸ τέλος, οὗ ἡ φρόνησις ἀληθὴς ὑπόληψίς ἐστιν.

It is possible to be good at deliberation quite simply, or to be good at deliberating in a particular domain. (In the one case you are right about how to realize the goal, with no further qualifications, and in the other you are right about how to realize a particular goal.) So, if deliberating well is characteristic of someone with *good judgment*, then *good deliberation* would be correctness about how to realize the goal that *good judgment* identifies correctly.

In chapters 10 and 11, Aristotle identifies two more virtues of action-oriented thinking, both of them closely related to good judgment (see figure 2 in the appendix). Then chapters 12 and 13 consider the importance of good judgment and scientific learning for human happiness.

[6.11]. . . . τί μὲν οὖν ἐστὶν ἡ φρόνησις καὶ ἡ σοφία, καὶ περὶ τί ἑκατέρα τυγχάνει οὖσα, καὶ ὅτι ἄλλου τῆς ψυχῆς μορίου ἀρετὴ ἑκατέρα, εἴρηται.

[6.12] Διαπορήσειε δ' ἄν τις περὶ αὐτῶν τί χρήσιμοί εἰσιν. ἡ μὲν γὰρ σοφία οὐδὲν θεωρήσει ἐξ ὧν ἔσται εὐδαίμων ἄνθρωπος (οὐδεμιᾶς γάρ ἐστι γενέσεως), ἡ δὲ φρόνησις τοῦτο μὲν ἔχει, ἀλλὰ τίνος ἕνεκα δεῖ αὐτῆς; εἴπερ ἡ μὲν φρόνησίς ἐστιν ἡ περὶ τὰ δίκαια καὶ καλὰ καὶ ἀγαθὰ ἀνθρώπῳ, ταῦτα δ' ἐστὶν ἃ τοῦ ἀγαθοῦ ἐστιν ἀνδρὸς πράττειν, οὐδὲν δὲ πρακτικώτεροι τῷ εἰδέναι αὐτά ἐσμεν, εἴπερ ἕξεις αἱ ἀρεταί εἰσιν, ὥσπερ οὐδὲ τὰ ὑγιεινὰ οὐδὲ τὰ εὐεκτικά, . . . οὐθὲν γὰρ πρακτικώτεροι τῷ ἔχειν τὴν ἰατρικὴν καὶ γυμναστικήν ἐσμεν. . . .

What Use Is Knowledge?

[6.11] . . . We have now stated what *good judgment* is, what *scientific learning* is, what their respective objects are, and that each is the virtue of a different part of the soul.

[6.12] Now someone might well wonder what use they are, since *scientific learning* isn't about any of the things that will make a human being happy (since it is not about anything that comes to be). And while *good judgment* does concern itself with such matters, what do we need it for? If it knows what actions are just and noble and good for humans to do, and these are what a good person will do, then knowing what they are won't make us any more likely to perform them—that is, if the virtues are dispositions to act. We can make the same point about healthy and wholesome behavior. . . . Having knowledge of medicine or athletics does not make us any more likely to engage in that behavior. . . .

πρὸς δὲ τούτοις ἄτοπον ἂν εἶναι δόξειεν, εἰ χείρων τῆς σοφίας οὖσα κυριωτέρα αὐτῆς ἔσται· ἡ γὰρ ποιοῦσα ἄρχει καὶ ἐπιτάττει περὶ ἕκαστον. περὶ δὴ τούτων λεκτέον· νῦν μὲν γὰρ ἠπόρηται περὶ αὐτῶν μόνον.

πρῶτον μὲν οὖν λέγωμεν ὅτι καθ᾽ αὑτὰς ἀναγκαῖον αἱρετὰς αὐτὰς εἶναι, ἀρετάς γ᾽ οὔσας ἑκατέραν ἑκατέρου τοῦ μορίου, καὶ εἰ μὴ ποιοῦσι μηδὲν μηδετέρα αὐτῶν. ἔπειτα καὶ ποιοῦσι μέν, οὐχ ὡς ἡ ἰατρικὴ δὲ ὑγίειαν, ἀλλ᾽ ὡς ἡ ὑγίεια, οὕτως ἡ σοφία εὐδαιμονίαν· μέρος γὰρ οὖσα τῆς ὅλης ἀρετῆς τῷ ἔχεσθαι ποιεῖ καὶ †τῷ ἐνεργεῖν εὐδαίμονα.† ἔτι τὸ ἔργον ἀποτελεῖται κατὰ τὴν φρόνησιν καὶ τὴν ἠθικὴν ἀρετήν· ἡ μὲν γὰρ ἀρετὴ τὸν σκοπὸν ποιεῖ ὀρθόν, ἡ δὲ φρόνησις τὰ πρὸς τοῦτον. . . .

It would also be odd if *good judgment*, which is subordinate to *scientific learning*, should be in charge of it, since what produces something rules over it and commands it. So let us take up these challenges, which so far we have only stated.

Let us reply, first, that both *good judgment* and *scientific learning* are choiceworthy in their own right—necessarily, since they are virtues, each of their respective part of the soul—even if nothing comes from either one. Next, we reply that something does come from them, although not in the way health comes from medicine; rather, *scientific learning* makes us happy in the way that health makes us healthy. It is part of virtue as a whole, and it makes us happy by our possession and exercise of it. Furthermore, we perform at our best by exercising both *good judgment* and virtue of character. Virtue makes the goal correct, while *good judgment* makes our pursuit of it correct. . . .

περὶ δὲ τοῦ μηθὲν εἶναι πρακτικωτέρους διὰ τὴν φρόνησιν τῶν καλῶν καὶ δικαίων, μικρὸν ἄνωθεν ἀρκτέον, λαβόντας ἀρχὴν ταύτην. ὥσπερ γὰρ καὶ τὰ δίκαια λέγομεν πράττοντάς τινας οὔπω δικαίους εἶναι, οἷον τοὺς τὰ ὑπὸ τῶν νόμων τεταγμένα ποιοῦντας ἢ ἄκοντας ἢ δι᾽ ἄγνοιαν ἢ δι᾽ ἕτερόν τι καὶ μὴ δι᾽ αὐτά (καίτοι πράττουσί γε ἃ δεῖ καὶ ὅσα χρὴ τὸν σπουδαῖον), οὕτως, ὡς ἔοικεν, ἔστι τὸ πῶς ἔχοντα πράττειν ἕκαστα ὥστ᾽ εἶναι ἀγαθόν, λέγω δ᾽ οἷον διὰ προαίρεσιν καὶ αὐτῶν ἕνεκα τῶν πραττομένων. τὴν μὲν οὖν προαίρεσιν ὀρθὴν ποιεῖ ἡ ἀρετή, τὸ δ᾽ ὅσα ἐκείνης ἕνεκα πέφυκε πράττεσθαι οὐκ ἔστι τῆς ἀρετῆς ἀλλ᾽ ἑτέρας δυνάμεως.

λεκτέον δ᾽ ἐπιστήσασι σαφέστερον περὶ αὐτῶν. ἔστι δὴ δύναμις ἣν καλοῦσι δεινότητα· αὕτη δ᾽ ἐστὶ τοιαύτη ὥστε τὰ πρὸς τὸν ὑποτεθέντα

As for the charge that *good judgment* does not make us any more likely to perform noble and just acts, we need to return to the principle we stated earlier. We say some people who perform just actions are not yet just people—for example, if they are simply doing what the laws command, or acting against their will, or acting because of ignorance or because of some other cause. They don't do what they do for its own sake, even though they do what they should, and what a good person must do. In the same way, it seems, it is also possible to perform these actions while meeting the criteria for being a good person. I mean, acting on purpose and choosing the actions for their own sake. While virtue makes your purpose correct, it is not the job of virtue but a different power to determine what actions to perform for the sake of that purpose.

Let us briefly clarify what those powers are. There is one power called cleverness, the ability to figure out and do what will promote a

σκοπὸν συντείνοντα δύνασθαι ταῦτα πράττειν καὶ τυγχάνειν αὐτῶν.³ ἂν μὲν οὖν ὁ σκοπὸς ᾖ καλός, ἐπαινετή ἐστιν, ἐὰν δὲ φαῦλος, πανουργία· ... ἔστι δ᾽ ἡ φρόνησις οὐχ ἡ δύναμις, ἀλλ᾽ οὐκ ἄνευ τῆς δυνάμεως ταύτης. ἡ δ᾽ ἕξις τῷ ὄμματι τούτῳ γίνεται τῆς ψυχῆς οὐκ ἄνευ ἀρετῆς, ὡς εἴρηταί τε καὶ ἔστι δῆλον· οἱ γὰρ συλλογισμοὶ τῶν πρακτῶν ἀρχὴν ἔχοντές εἰσιν, ἐπειδὴ τοιόνδε τὸ τέλος καὶ τὸ ἄριστον, ὁτιδήποτε ὄν ... τοῦτο δ᾽ εἰ μὴ τῷ ἀγαθῷ, οὐ φαίνεται· διαστρέφει γὰρ ἡ μοχθηρία καὶ διαψεύδεσθαι ποιεῖ περὶ τὰς πρακτικὰς ἀρχάς. ὥστε φανερὸν ὅτι ἀδύνατον φρόνιμον εἶναι μὴ ὄντα ἀγαθόν.

[6.13] Σκεπτέον δὴ πάλιν καὶ περὶ ἀρετῆς· καὶ γὰρ ἡ ἀρετὴ παραπλησίως ἔχει ὡς ἡ φρόνησις πρὸς τὴν δεινότητα—οὐ ταὐτὸ μέν, ὅμοιον δέ—οὕτω

given objective. It is praiseworthy when your objective is noble, but mere resourcefulness when you aim to do something bad. . . . *Good judgment* is not the same power as cleverness, although it does involve it. The soul does not develop keen eyesight without virtue—as we have already made clear. That's because reasoning about what to do starts from the principle that *such and such is the goal and is best*—whatever that may be. . . . This principle, however, is evident only to a good person, since vice distorts and falsifies the principles of our actions. Thus it is impossible to have *good judgment* without also being a good person.

Natural and Genuine Virtue

[6.13] Now, back to the subject of virtue. Like good judgment, it has a counterpart that is similar to it but distinct from it. This is natural virtue, which is like genuine virtue in the same way

καὶ ἡ φυσικὴ ἀρετὴ πρὸς τὴν κυρίαν. πᾶσι γὰρ δοκεῖ ἕκαστα τῶν ἠθῶν ὑπάρχειν φύσει πως· καὶ γὰρ δίκαιοι καὶ σωφρονικοὶ καὶ ἀνδρεῖοι καὶ τἆλλα ἔχομεν εὐθὺς ἐκ γενετῆς· ἀλλ’ ὅμως ζητοῦμεν ἕτερόν τι τὸ κυρίως ἀγαθὸν καὶ τὰ τοιαῦτα ἄλλον τρόπον ὑπάρχειν. καὶ γὰρ παισὶ καὶ θηρίοις αἱ φυσικαὶ ὑπάρχουσιν ἕξεις, ἀλλ’ ἄνευ νοῦ βλαβεραὶ φαίνονται οὖσαι. πλὴν τοσοῦτον ἔοικεν ὁρᾶσθαι, ὅτι ὥσπερ σώματι ἰσχυρῷ ἄνευ ὄψεως κινουμένῳ συμβαίνει σφάλλεσθαι ἰσχυρῶς διὰ τὸ μὴ ἔχειν ὄψιν, οὕτω καὶ ἐνταῦθα· ἐὰν δὲ λάβῃ νοῦν, ἐν τῷ πράττειν διαφέρει· ἡ δ’ ἕξις ὁμοία οὖσα τότ’ ἔσται κυρίως ἀρετή. ὥστε καθάπερ ἐπὶ τοῦ δοξαστικοῦ δύο ἐστὶν εἴδη, δεινότης καὶ φρόνησις, οὕτω καὶ ἐπὶ τοῦ ἠθικοῦ δύο ἐστί, τὸ μὲν ἀρετὴ φυσικὴ τὸ δ’ ἡ κυρία, καὶ τούτων ἡ κυρία οὐ γίνεται ἄνευ φρονήσεως. . . .

good judgment is like cleverness. It is apparent to everyone that the various types of character can be natural in a way. For example we can be just, disciplined, brave, and so on, right from birth. But the genuine goodness that is the object of our inquiry is a different version of these traits. The natural dispositions can be found in children and wild animals but are clearly harmful when intelligence is not involved. The same thing can likely be observed in their case as happens to a powerful body moving around without sight, when it stumbles badly because it cannot see. If you acquire intelligence, however, it makes a difference to how you act, and your disposition will be not just similar to virtue but genuinely a virtue. We conclude that just as there are two dispositions of mind, cleverness and *good judgment*, there are also two kinds of character traits, natural virtue and genuine virtue, and the genuine kind does not arise without *good judgment*. . . .

δῆλον δέ, κἂν εἰ μὴ πρακιική ἦν, ὅτι ἔδει ἂν αὐτῆς διὰ τὸ τοῦ μορίου ἀρετὴν εἶναι, καὶ ὅτι οὐκ ἔσται ἡ προαίρεσις ὀρθὴ ἄνευ φρονήσεως οὐδ' ἄνευ ἀρετῆς· ἡ μὲν γὰρ τὸ τέλος ἡ δὲ τὰ πρὸς τὸ τέλος ποιεῖ πράττειν. ἀλλὰ μὴν οὐδὲ κυρία γ' ἐστὶ τῆς σοφίας οὐδὲ τοῦ βελτίονος μορίου, ὥσπερ οὐδὲ τῆς ὑγιείας ἡ ἰατρική· οὐ γὰρ χρῆται αὐτῇ, ἀλλ' ὁρᾷ ὅπως γένηται· ἐκείνης οὖν ἕνεκα

Aristotle now pauses to contrast his own view with claims that Socrates made about the relation between virtue of character and good judgment, and about whether it is possible to have one virtue without having them all. This is possible only for the natural virtues, not the genuine virtues of character, Aristotle maintains. He then returns to conclude his response to the objections introduced at the beginning of chapter 12.

Clearly, even if *good judgment* didn't result in action, we would still need it, since it is a part of virtue. Is also clear that our choices will not be correct without good judgment—or without virtue, since the one supplies the goal while the other makes us act to realize the goal. Moreover, *good judgment* is not in charge of *scientific learning*, or of the better part of the soul—any more than medicine is in charge of health. Medicine does not *employ* health; it sees that it comes into being. So too with good

ἐπιτάττει, ἀλλ' οὐκ ἐκείνη. ἔτι ὅμοιον κἂν εἴ τις τὴν πολιτικὴν φαίη ἄρχειν τῶν θεῶν, ὅτι ἐπιτάττει περὶ πάντα τὰ ἐν τῇ πόλει.

judgment: it does not issue orders *to* scientific learning, but *on its behalf*. It is as if someone objected that the *art of politics* rules over the gods because it gives orders about everything in the city.

[7.1] Μετὰ δὲ ταῦτα λεκτέον, ἄλλην ποιησαμέ-
νους ἀρχήν, ὅτι τῶν περὶ τὰ ἤθη φευκτῶν τρία
ἐστὶν εἴδη, κακία ἀκρασία θηριότης. τὰ δ' ἐναντία
τοῖς μὲν δυσὶ δῆλα· τὸ μὲν γὰρ ἀρετὴν τὸ δ'
ἐγκράτειαν καλοῦμεν· πρὸς δὲ τὴν θηριότητα

6. LOSING CONTROL

(Book 7)

Vice, Loss of Control, and Beastliness

Aristotle now turns to the familiar phenomenon of struggling to do what you think is right. He has a single term for losing the struggle (AKRASIA) and a single term for winning it (ENKRATEIA). One of his goals is to explain how akrasia is different from the vice of self-indulgence, and how enkrateia is different from the virtue of self-discipline.

[7.1] Next let us take a different tack and note that in matters of character, there are three kinds of thing to be avoided: vice, losing control, and beastliness. The opposites of the first two are clear; we call them virtue and self-control,

μάλιστ' ἂν ἁρμόττοι λέγειν τὴν ὑπὲρ ἡμᾶς ἀρετήν, ἡρωικήν τινα καὶ θείαν . . . ἀλλὰ περὶ μὲν τῆς δια-θέσεως τῆς τοιαύτης ὕστερον ποιητέον τινὰ μνείαν, περὶ δὲ κακίας εἴρηται πρότερον· περὶ δὲ ἀκρασίας καὶ μαλακίας καὶ τρυφῆς λεκτέον, καὶ περὶ ἐγκρατείας καὶ καρτερίας· οὔτε γὰρ ὡς περὶ τῶν αὐτῶν ἕξεων τῇ ἀρετῇ καὶ τῇ μοχθηρίᾳ ἑκατέραν αὐτῶν ὑποληπτέον, οὔθ' ὡς ἕτερον γένος. . . .

Δοκεῖ δὴ ἥ τε ἐγκράτεια καὶ καρτερία τῶν σπουδαίων καὶ [τῶν] ἐπαινετῶν εἶναι, ἡ δ' ἀκρα-σία τε καὶ μαλακία τῶν φαύλων καὶ ψεκτῶν, καὶ ὁ αὐτὸς ἐγκρατὴς καὶ ἐμμενετικὸς τῷ λογισμῷ, καὶ ἀκρατὴς καὶ ἐκστατικὸς τοῦ λογισμοῦ. καὶ ὁ μὲν ἀκρατὴς εἰδὼς ὅτι φαῦλα πράττει διὰ πάθος, ὁ δ' ἐγκρατὴς εἰδὼς ὅτι φαῦλαι αἱ ἐπιθυμίαι οὐκ ἀκολουθεῖ διὰ τὸν λόγον. . . .

respectively. As for the opposite of beastliness, the best fit would be a superhuman virtue, something heroic and divine. . . . We won't say any more about beastliness until later, and we have already discussed vice. So now let us discuss losing control, weakness, and softness, as well as self-control and toughness. None of these is the same condition as virtue or vice, but they are not in a different category, either. . . .

Here is what seems to the case. When you exercise self-control and are tough, that is good and praiseworthy. When you lose control and are weak, that is bad and blameworthy. When you exercise self-control, you stick to your judgment. When you lose control, you abandon your judgment. When you lose control, you know that what you are doing is wrong, but you do it anyway because of your feelings. When you exercise self-control you know that your feelings of attraction are bad and you resist following them because of your judgment. . . .

[7.3] . . . οὔτε γὰρ περὶ ἄπαντ' ἐστὶν ὁ ἁπλῶς ἀκρατής, ἀλλὰ περὶ ἅπερ ὁ ἀκόλαστος, οὔτε τῷ πρὸς ταῦτα ἁπλῶς ἔχειν (ταὐτὸν γὰρ ἂν ἦν τῇ ἀκολασίᾳ), ἀλλὰ τῷ ὡδὶ ἔχειν. ὃ μὲν γὰρ ἄγεται προαιρούμενος, νομίζων ἀεὶ δεῖν τὸ παρὸν ἡδὺ διώκειν· ὃ δ' οὐκ οἴεται μέν, διώκει δέ. . . .

Aristotle notes that it is disputed whether akra-sia is the same as SELF-INDULGENCE *(a vice of character) and whether it is possible for an akratic person to have* GOOD JUDGMENT *(a virtue of intellect) and really know that what they are doing is wrong. He offers his own resolution to these disputes starting in chapter 3.*

[7.3] . . . It is not over just anything that we say people lose control (not in the ordinary sense of the phrase). It has to be over the sorts of things that attract self-indulgent people. And it is not simply a matter of being attracted to those things; otherwise it would be the same as self-indulgence.[27] Rather, you have to relate to them in a particular way: if you are self-indulgent you *choose* to pursue the thing that attracts you and always think you should pursue the present pleasure. If you are the other type, you don't think you should pursue it, but you go for it nonetheless. . . .

. . . ἐπεὶ διχῶς λέγομεν τὸ ἐπίστασθαι (καὶ γὰρ ὁ ἔχων μὲν οὐ χρώμενος δὲ τῇ ἐπιστήμῃ καὶ ὁ χρώμενος λέγεται ἐπίστασθαι), διοίσει τὸ ἔχοντα μὲν μὴ θεωροῦντα δὲ καὶ τὸ θεωροῦντα ἃ μὴ δεῖ πράττειν [τοῦ ἔχοντα καὶ θεωροῦντα]· τοῦτο γὰρ δοκεῖ δεινόν, ἀλλ' οὐκ εἰ μὴ θεωρῶν. . . .

τὸ δὲ λέγειν τοὺς λόγους τοὺς ἀπὸ τῆς ἐπιστήμης οὐδὲν σημεῖον· καὶ γὰρ οἱ ἐν τοῖς πάθεσι τούτοις ὄντες ἀποδείξεις καὶ ἔπη λέγουσιν

Knowingly Doing Wrong

. . . Now there are two different situations in which we attribute knowledge to people; we say someone knows something both when they have the knowledge but are not using it, and when they are using it. So, it will make a difference whether we maintain that people do what is wrong while knowing *but not actively thinking* that it is wrong, or we maintain that they do what is wrong *while actively thinking* that it is wrong. The latter would seem strange, but not the former. . . .

After some examples, Aristotle anticipates the objection that akratic agents do actively know that what they are doing is wrong, since they say this while they are acting. He responds.
Just because they utter words of knowledge does not mean that they know what they are saying. For example, people in the throes of passion recite proofs and verses of Empedocles,[28]

Ἐμπεδοκλέους, καὶ οἱ πρῶτον μαθόντες συν-
είρουσι μὲν τοὺς λόγους, ἴσασι δ᾽ οὔπω· . . .
ὥστε καθάπερ τοὺς ὑποκρινομένους, οὕτως
ὑποληπτέον λέγειν καὶ τοὺς ἀκρατευομένους.

ἔτι καὶ ὧδε φυσικῶς ἄν τις ἐπιβλέψειε τὴν αἰτίαν.
ἢ μὲν γὰρ καθόλου δόξα, ἡ δ᾽ ἑτέρα περὶ τῶν καθ᾽
ἕκαστά ἐστιν, ὧν αἴσθησις ἤδη κυρία· ὅταν δὲ μία
γένηται ἐξ αὐτῶν, ἀνάγκη τὸ συμπερανθὲν ἔνθα
μὲν φάναι τὴν ψυχήν, ἐν δὲ ταῖς ποιητικαῖς πράττειν εὐθύς· οἷον, εἰ παντὸς γλυκέος γεύεσθαι δεῖ,
τουτὶ δὲ γλυκὺ ὡς ἕν τι τῶν καθ᾽ ἕκαστον, ἀνάγκη τὸν δυνάμενον καὶ μὴ κωλυόμενον ἅμα τοῦτο
καὶ πράττειν. ὅταν οὖν ἡ μὲν καθόλου ἐνῇ κω-
λύουσα γεύεσθαι, ἡ δέ, ὅτι πᾶν γλυκὺ ἡδύ, τουτὶ
δὲ γλυκύ (αὕτη δὲ ἐνεργεῖ), τύχῃ δ᾽ ἐπιθυμία

and beginners learning a subject string together the words, but don't yet understand them. . . . This is how we should construe what people are saying when they lose control; they are like actors reciting lines.

What Happens When We Lose Control

Furthermore, from a scientific perspective, we might offer the following explanation. One kind of belief is universal, while another is about particulars, which are judged by perception. When we infer from them a single conclusion, it is necessary that the soul both affirm it and straightaway act on it. For example, if we should taste anything sweet, and this particular thing is sweet, and we are able to taste it and are not impeded, necessarily that's what we do. But consider what happens when a universal belief forbids tasting, yet another belief says that everything sweet is pleasant, and that this particular thing is sweet. The latter belief is

ἐνοῦσα, ἣ μὲν οὖν λέγει φεύγειν τοῦτο, ἡ δ' ἐπιθυμία ἄγει· κινεῖν γὰρ ἕκαστον δύναται τῶν
μορίων· . . .

active, and we actually feel the appetite. In that case, the one belief says to avoid the sweet, but the appetite draws us toward it, since it has the power to move each part of our body. . . .

The following chapters of book 7 consider a different version of akrasia: being unable to control your temper when provoked. Then Aristotle addresses the relation between akrasia and virtue and denies that an akratic can have good judgment. The closing chapters of the book address the nature and value of pleasure, a task Aristotle will also take up in book 10.

[8.1] Μετὰ δὲ ταῦτα περὶ φιλίας ἔποιτ' ἂν διελθεῖν· ἔστι γὰρ ἀρετή τις ἢ μετ' ἀρετῆς, ἔτι δ' ἀναγκαιότατον εἰς τὸν βίον. ἄνευ γὰρ φίλων οὐδεὶς ἕλοιτ' ἂν ζῆν, ἔχων τὰ λοιπὰ ἀγαθὰ πάντα· καὶ γὰρ πλουτοῦσι καὶ ἀρχὰς καὶ δυναστείας κεκτημένοις δοκεῖ φίλων μάλιστ' εἶναι χρεία· τί γὰρ ὄφελος τῆς τοιαύτης εὐετηρίας ἀφαιρεθείσης εὐεργεσίας, ἣ γίγνεται μάλιστα καὶ ἐπαινετωτάτη πρὸς φίλους; ἢ πῶς ἂν τηρηθείη καὶ

7. FRIENDSHIP AND THE GOOD LIFE

(Books 8 and 9)

Why Have Friends?

[8.1] Our next task would be to examine friendship. That's because friendship is a virtue, or connected to virtue. Also, it is utterly indispensable in life. No one would choose to live without friends, even if they had all the other good things in life. Indeed, rich people and those in positions of power and authority seem to need friends most of all. After all, what use is such prosperity if you cannot be a benefactor? And that is something you do especially, and most commendably, to your friends. Besides, how would such prosperity be maintained and

σῴζοιτ' ἄνευ φίλων; ὅσῳ γὰρ πλείων, τοσούτῳ ἐπισφαλεστέρα.

ἐν πενίᾳ τε καὶ ταῖς λοιπαῖς δυστυχίαις μόνην οἴονται καταφυγὴν εἶναι τοὺς φίλους. καὶ νέοις δὲ πρὸς τὸ ἀναμάρτητον καὶ πρεσβυτέροις πρὸς θεραπείαν καὶ τὸ ἐλλεῖπον τῆς πράξεως δι' ἀσθένειαν βοηθείας, τοῖς τ' ἐν ἀκμῇ πρὸς τὰς καλὰς πράξεις· "σύν τε δύ' ἐρχομένω·" καὶ γὰρ νοῆσαι καὶ πρᾶξαι δυνατώτεροι.

φύσει τ' ἐνυπάρχειν ἔοικε πρὸς τὸ γεγεννημένον τῷ γεννήσαντι καὶ πρὸς τὸ γεννῆσαν τῷ γεννηθέντι, οὐ μόνον ἐν ἀνθρώποις ἀλλὰ καὶ ἐν ὄρνισι καὶ τοῖς πλείστοις τῶν ζῴων, καὶ τοῖς ὁμοεθνέσι πρὸς ἄλληλα, καὶ μάλιστα τοῖς ἀνθρώποις, ὅθεν τοὺς φιλανθρώπους ἐπαινοῦμεν. ἴδοι δ' ἄν τις καὶ ἐν ταῖς πλάναις ὡς οἰκεῖον ἅπας ἄνθρωπος ἀνθρώπῳ καὶ φίλον. ἔοικε δὲ καὶ τὰς πόλεις συνέχειν ἡ φιλία, καὶ οἱ νομοθέται μᾶλλον περὶ αὐτὴν σπουδάζειν ἢ τὴν δικαιοσύνην· ἡ γὰρ

FRIENDSHIP AND THE GOOD LIFE

preserved without friends? The greater your prosperity, the more precarious it is.

In poverty or other kinds of misfortune, our only refuge seems to be our friends. The young need friends to keep them from error. The old need friends to take care of them and assist them in matters where their power of action is diminished. People in the prime of life need friends if they are to accomplish noble deeds: "when two go forth together" they are mightier in thought and action.[29]

Nature makes parents friends to their offspring, and offspring friends to their parents — not only among humans but also among birds and most animals. It makes members of the same species friends to each other. This is especially the case among humans, which is why we praise people for their love of humanity. Wayfarers, too, are likely to observe the kinship that any human being feels for another. Even cities are held together by friendship, it seems, and legislators place more importance on it even

ὁμόνοια ὅμοιόν τι τῇ φιλίᾳ ἔοικεν εἶναι, ταύτης
δὲ μάλιστ᾽ ἐφίενται καὶ τὴν στάσιν ἔχθραν οὖσαν
μάλιστα ἐξελαύνουσιν· καὶ φίλων μὲν ὄντων
οὐδὲν δεῖ δικαιοσύνης, δίκαιοι δ᾽ ὄντες προσδέον-
ται φιλίας, καὶ τῶν δικαίων τὸ μάλιστα φιλικὸν
εἶναι δοκεῖ. . . .

[8.2] Τάχα δ᾽ ἂν γένοιτο περὶ αὐτῶν φανερὸν
γνωρισθέντος τοῦ φιλητοῦ. δοκεῖ γὰρ οὐ πᾶν φι-
λεῖσθαι ἀλλὰ τὸ φιλητόν, τοῦτο δ᾽ εἶναι ἀγαθὸν ἢ
ἡδὺ ἢ χρήσιμον· δόξειε δ᾽ ἂν χρήσιμον εἶναι δι᾽

than on justice. Concord, which seems quite similar to friendship, is what they strive most of all to cultivate, and conflict, a form of enmity, is what they seek most of all to drive out. Although people have no need for justice when they are friends, just people still need friends; and especially just acts seem to be friendly. . . .

After addressing some puzzles about friendship (some of which can be found in Plato's LYSIS), Aristotle distinguishes three main forms of friendship, based on three different objects of love.

THREE THINGS WE LOVE

[8.2] Perhaps we can gain clarity on these matters by identifying the object of love. It seems we don't love just anything; we love things that are lovable, and these are good, pleasant, or useful. We think something is useful if

οὗ γίνεται ἀγαθόν τι ἢ ἡδονή, ὥστε φιλητὰ ἂν εἴη τἀγαθόν τε καὶ τὸ ἡδὺ ὡς τέλη. . . .

ἐπὶ μὲν τῇ τῶν ἀψύχων φιλήσει οὐ λέγεται φιλία· οὐ γάρ ἐστιν ἀντιφίλησις, οὐδὲ βούλησις ἐκείνῳ ἀγαθοῦ (γελοῖον γὰρ ἴσως τῷ οἴνῳ βούλεσθαι τἀγαθά, ἀλλ᾽ εἴπερ, σῴζεσθαι βούλεται αὐτόν, ἵνα αὐτὸς ἔχῃ)· τῷ δὲ φίλῳ φασὶ δεῖν βούλεσθαι τἀγαθὰ ἐκείνου ἕνεκα. τοὺς δὲ βουλομένους οὕτω τἀγαθὰ εὔνους λέγουσιν, ἂν μὴ ταὐτὸ καὶ παρ᾽ ἐκείνου γίνηται· εὔνοιαν γὰρ ἐν ἀντιπεπονθόσι φιλίαν εἶναι. ἢ προσθετέον μὴ λανθάνουσαν; πολλοὶ γάρ εἰσιν εὖνοι οἷς οὐχ ἑωράκασιν, ὑπολαμβάνουσι δὲ ἐπιεικεῖς εἶναι ἢ χρησίμους· . . .

δεῖ ἄρα εὐνοεῖν ἀλλήλοις καὶ βούλεσθαι τἀγαθὰ μὴ λανθάνοντας δι᾽ ἕν τι τῶν εἰρημένων.

it has a good result or brings us pleasure, so the ultimate objects of love would be the good and the pleasant. . . .

Love of an inanimate object isn't called friendship, since the love is not reciprocated and you do not wish good to the object. For example, it would be silly to wish good to the wine, except insofar as you want to preserve and keep it yourself. But you must wish good things to a friend, people say, and for the friend's own sake. When you wish good in this way, but the other person does not reciprocate, people say you have goodwill; when goodwill is reciprocated, they call it friendship. Do we need to add that friends are aware of the goodwill? Many of us have goodwill toward people we have never seen but consider decent or useful. . . .

The upshot is that friends must have mutual goodwill—for one of the three reasons we mentioned—and they must be aware of that goodwill.

[8.3] . . . τρία δὴ τὰ τῆς φιλίας εἴδη, ἰσάριθμα τοῖς φιλητοῖς· καθ᾽ ἕκαστον γάρ ἐστιν ἀντιφίλησις οὐ λανθάνουσα, οἱ δὲ φιλοῦντες ἀλλήλους βούλονται τἀγαθὰ ἀλλήλοις ταύτῃ ᾗ φιλοῦσιν.

οἱ μὲν οὖν διὰ τὸ χρήσιμον φιλοῦντες ἀλλήλους οὐ καθ᾽ αὑτοὺς φιλοῦσιν, ἀλλ᾽ ᾗ γίνεταί τι αὐτοῖς παρ᾽ ἀλλήλων ἀγαθόν. ὁμοίως δὲ καὶ οἱ δι᾽ ἡδονήν· οὐ γὰρ τῷ ποιούς τινας εἶναι ἀγαπῶσι τοὺς εὐτραπέλους, ἀλλ᾽ ὅτι ἡδεῖς αὐτοῖς. οἵ τε δὴ διὰ τὸ χρήσιμον φιλοῦντες διὰ τὸ αὐτοῖς ἀγαθὸν στέργουσι, καὶ οἱ δι᾽ ἡδονὴν διὰ τὸ αὐτοῖς ἡδύ, καὶ οὐχ ᾗ ὁ φιλούμενός ἐστιν, ἀλλ᾽ ᾗ χρήσιμος ἢ ἡδύς. . . . εὐδιάλυτοι δὴ αἱ τοιαῦταί εἰσι, μὴ

THREE FORMS OF FRIENDSHIP

[8.3] . . . There are three forms of friendship, the same number as the objects of love. In each case, the love is recognized and reciprocated; and insofar as the friends love each other they wish each other well.

Friends whose love is based on utility love each other not in their own right, but insofar as they get something good from each other. The same is true for those who love another person because of pleasure. They find amusing people congenial, not for having a particular character, but for giving them pleasure. People who love another person based on utility feel affection for the other because of what is good to themselves, and people who love another because of pleasure feel affection for the other because of what is pleasant to themselves. Their love depends not on the loved person's being who they are, but on their being pleasant or useful. . . . Such friendships are easily dissolved when the people

διαμενόντων αὐτῶν ὁμοίων· ἐὰν γὰρ μηκέτι
ἡδεῖς ἢ χρήσιμοι ὦσι, παύονται φιλοῦντες.

τὸ δὲ χρήσιμον οὐ διαμένει, ἀλλ᾽ ἄλλοτε ἄλλο
γίνεται. ἀπολυθέντος οὖν δι᾽ ὃ φίλοι ἦσαν, δια-
λύεται καὶ ἡ φιλία, ὡς οὔσης τῆς φιλίας πρὸς
ἐκεῖνα. μάλιστα δ᾽ ἐν τοῖς πρεσβύταις ἡ τοιαύτη
δοκεῖ φιλία γίνεσθαι (οὐ γὰρ τὸ ἡδὺ οἱ τηλικοῦτοι
διώκουσιν ἀλλὰ τὸ ὠφέλιμον) . . . οὐ πάνυ δ᾽ οἱ
τοιοῦτοι οὐδὲ συζῶσι μετ᾽ ἀλλήλων· ἐνίοτε γὰρ
οὐδ᾽ εἰσὶν ἡδεῖς· . . .

ἡ δὲ τῶν νέων φιλία δι᾽ ἡδονὴν εἶναι δοκεῖ·
κατὰ πάθος γὰρ οὗτοι ζῶσι, καὶ μάλιστα διώκουσι
τὸ ἡδὺ αὐτοῖς καὶ τὸ παρόν· τῆς ἡλικίας δὲ μετα-
πιπτούσης καὶ τὰ ἡδέα γίνεται ἕτερα. διὸ ταχέως
γίνονται φίλοι καὶ παύονται· ἅμα γὰρ τῷ ἡδεῖ ἡ
φιλία μεταπίπτει, τῆς δὲ τοιαύτης ἡδονῆς ταχεῖα
ἡ μεταβολή. . . . συνημερεύειν δὲ καὶ συζῆν οὗτοι

in them change. If they are no longer pleasant or useful, they stop being friends.

Utility tends not to endure. It alters over time, and once the basis of the friendship is destroyed, so is the friendship that depends on it. This kind of friendship is found mainly among the old, since people that age tend to purse what benefits them rather than what is pleasant. . . . Friends of this sort tend not to live together; and sometimes they don't even enjoy each other's company. . . .

Friendship among the young seems to be based on pleasure. Young people live by their passions and mostly pursue what is pleasant to them and immediately available. At this inconstant stage of life, what pleases a person will fluctuate as well. That is why people become friends quickly at this age, and quickly stop being friends, since their love alters along with their pleasures. . . . Friends of this sort do wish to spend their days together and live together,

βούλονται· γίνεται γὰρ αὐτοῖς τὸ κατὰ τὴν φιλίαν οὕτως.

Τελεία δ᾽ ἐστὶν ἡ τῶν ἀγαθῶν φιλία καὶ κατ᾽ ἀρετὴν ὁμοίων· οὗτοι γὰρ τἀγαθὰ ὁμοίως βούλονται ἀλλήλοις ᾗ ἀγαθοί, ἀγαθοὶ δ᾽ εἰσὶ καθ᾽ αὑτούς. οἱ δὲ βουλόμενοι τἀγαθὰ τοῖς φίλοις ἐκείνων ἕνεκα μάλιστα φίλοι· . . .

διαμένει οὖν ἡ τούτων φιλία ἕως ἂν ἀγαθοὶ ὦσιν, ἡ δ᾽ ἀρετὴ μόνιμον. καὶ ἔστιν ἑκάτερος ἁπλῶς ἀγαθὸς καὶ τῷ φίλῳ. . . . ὁμοίως δὲ καὶ ἡδεῖς· καὶ γὰρ ἁπλῶς οἱ ἀγαθοὶ ἡδεῖς καὶ ἀλλήλοις· ἑκάστῳ γὰρ καθ᾽ ἡδονήν εἰσιν αἱ οἰκεῖαι πράξεις καὶ αἱ τοιαῦται, τῶν ἀγαθῶν δὲ αἱ αὐταὶ ἢ ὅμοιαι. ἡ τοιαύτη δὲ φιλία μόνιμος εὐλόγως ἐστίν· συνάπτει γὰρ ἐν αὐτῇ πάνθ᾽ ὅσα τοῖς φίλοις δεῖ ὑπάρχειν . . .

since that is how they reap the fruits of the friendship.

When the friends are good people of comparable virtue, their friendship is complete. They wish each other well, just insofar as they are good, and they are good in their own right. To wish your friends well for the friends' own sake is friendship in the fullest sense. . . .

Friendship between people of this sort endures as long as the parties remain good, and virtue is an enduring thing. Each party is simply good, and also good to their friend. . . . And they are likewise pleasant, since good people are simply pleasant, as well as pleasant to each other (that's because anyone enjoys their own proper actions—and actions of that sort—and good people perform the same kind of actions as each other, or similar ones). It is not surprising that friendship of this kind is enduring, since it includes all the features necessary for friendship. . . .

καὶ τὸ φιλεῖν δὴ καὶ ἡ φιλία ἐν τούτοις μάλιστα καὶ ἀρίστη. σπανίας δ᾽ εἰκὸς τὰς τοιαύτας
εἶναι· ὀλίγοι γὰρ οἱ τοιοῦτοι. ἔτι δὲ προσδεῖται
χρόνου καὶ συνηθείας· κατὰ τὴν παροιμίαν γὰρ
οὐκ ἔστιν εἰδῆσαι ἀλλήλους πρὶν τοὺς λεγομένους
ἅλας συναναλῶσαι· οὐδ᾽ ἀποδέξασθαι δὴ πρότερον οὐδ᾽ εἶναι φίλους, πρὶν ἂν ἑκάτερος ἑκατέρῳ
φανῇ φιλητὸς καὶ πιστευθῇ. οἱ δὲ ταχέως τὰ φι-
λικὰ πρὸς ἀλλήλους ποιοῦντες βούλονται μὲν
φίλοι εἶναι, οὐκ εἰσὶ δέ, εἰ μὴ καὶ φιλητοί, καὶ τοῦτ᾽
ἴσασιν· βούλησις μὲν γὰρ ταχεῖα φιλίας γίνεται,
φιλία δ᾽ οὔ.

It is especially among people of this sort that one finds the best love and friendship, but it is rare, since such people are few and far between. It also takes time to develop and requires familiarity, since people can't know each other until they have consumed together the proverbial quantity of salt. They will not find each other congenial or be friends until each is dear to and trusted by the other. People who quickly become friendly may *want* to be friends, but they are not. While the wish to be friends arises quickly, friendship itself does not.

In later chapters of book 8, Aristotle discusses factors that may strain a friendship. These include living apart and various kinds of inequality. In book 9, he focuses mainly on friendship between good people. In chapter 9, he asks whether we need friends to be happy.

[9.9] Ἀμφισβητεῖται δὲ καὶ περὶ τὸν εὐδαίμονα, εἰ δεήσεται φίλων ἢ μή. οὐθὲν γάρ φασι δεῖν φίλων τοῖς μακαρίοις καὶ αὐτάρκεσιν· ὑπάρχειν γὰρ αὐτοῖς τἀγαθά· αὐτάρκεις οὖν ὄντας οὐδενὸς προσδεῖσθαι, τὸν δὲ φίλον, ἕτερον αὐτὸν ὄντα, πορίζειν ἃ δι᾿ αὑτοῦ ἀδυνατεῖ· ὅθεν "ὅταν ὁ δαίμων εὖ διδῷ, τί δεῖ φίλων;"

ἔοικε δ᾿ ἀτόπῳ τὸ πάντ᾿ ἀπονέμοντας τἀγαθὰ τῷ εὐδαίμονι φίλους μὴ ἀποδιδόναι, ὃ δοκεῖ τῶν ἐκτὸς ἀγαθῶν μέγιστον εἶναι. εἴ τε φίλου μᾶλλόν ἐστι τὸ εὖ ποιεῖν ἢ πάσχειν, καὶ ἔστι τοῦ ἀγαθοῦ καὶ τῆς ἀρετῆς τὸ εὐεργετεῖν, κάλλιον δ᾿ εὖ

Does a Happy Person Need Friends?

[9.9] There is also a dispute about whether a happy person will need friends. One side claims that anyone who is blessed and self-sufficient has no need of friends, since they already have what is good. If you are self-sufficient, they say, you don't need anything else, and a friend—your other self—provides what you can't provide for yourself—hence the saying: "If you are well endowed by god, what need do you have for friends?"

But it would be strange for the god to bestow upon the happy person every good thing *except* friends, which are considered to be the greatest external good. If being a friend is more about benefitting others than being benefitted, and conferring benefits is characteristic of a good person and a mark of virtue; and if it is nobler to do good to your friends than to do good to strangers, then good people will need to have

ποιεῖν φίλους ὀθνείων, τῶν εὖ πεισομένων δεήσεται ὁ σπουδαῖος . . .

ἄτοπον δ᾽ ἴσως καὶ τὸ μονώτην ποιεῖν τὸν μα-
κάριον· οὐδεὶς γὰρ ἕλοιτ᾽ ἂν καθ᾽ αὑτὸν τὰ πάντ᾽
ἔχειν ἀγαθά· πολιτικὸν γὰρ ὁ ἄνθρωπος καὶ συζῆν
πεφυκός. καὶ τῷ εὐδαίμονι δὴ τοῦθ᾽ ὑπάρχει· τὰ
γὰρ τῇ φύσει ἀγαθὰ ἔχει, δῆλον δ᾽ ὡς μετὰ φίλων
καὶ ἐπιεικῶν κρεῖττον ἢ μετ᾽ ὀθνείων καὶ τῶν
τυχόντων συνημερεύειν. δεῖ ἄρα τῷ εὐδαίμονι
φίλων. . . .

ὡς δὲ πρὸς ἑαυτὸν ἔχει ὁ σπουδαῖος, καὶ πρὸς
τὸν φίλον (ἕτερος γὰρ αὐτὸς ὁ φίλος ἐστίν)· καθάπερ οὖν τὸ αὑτὸν εἶναι αἱρετόν ἐστιν ἑκάστῳ,
οὕτω καὶ τὸ τὸν φίλον, ἢ παραπλησίως. τὸ δ᾽ εἶναι
ἦν αἱρετὸν διὰ τὸ αἰσθάνεσθαι αὑτοῦ ἀγαθοῦ
ὄντος, ἡ δὲ τοιαύτη αἴσθησις ἡδεῖα καθ᾽ ἑαυτήν.
συναισθάνεσθαι ἄρα δεῖ καὶ τοῦ φίλου ὅτι ἔστιν,
τοῦτο δὲ γίνοιτ᾽ ἂν ἐν τῷ συζῆν καὶ κοινωνεῖν

friends to be the recipients of these good deeds. . . .

It is also strange to construe the happy person as a solitary creature, for no one would choose to have all good things on their own. Human beings are social creatures, whose nature is to live in company with others, and the same is true of a happy person. For what is naturally good belongs to them, and it is clearly better to spend your days in the company of friends and good people than in the company of strangers or just anyone. So a happy person will need to have friends. . . .

If you are a good person, you stand in the same relation to your friend as to yourself, since a friend is another self. You value your friend's existence in the same way as you value your own, or almost. Existing is valuable to you because of the pleasure of perceiving your own goodness, and your friend's existence needs to be included in that awareness. You get that shared awareness from a shared life, from

λόγων καὶ διανοίας· οὕτω γὰρ ἂν δόξειε τὸ συζῆν
ἐπὶ τῶν ἀνθρώπων λέγεσθαι, καὶ οὐχ ὥσπερ ἐπὶ
τῶν βοσκημάτων τὸ ἐν τῷ αὐτῷ νέμεσθαι. . . .

conversation, and from thinking together. That is what is meant by a shared life in the case of human beings, which is not like the life of grazing animals who feed in the same pasture. . . .

Aristotle goes on to ask how many friends a person needs—it depends on what type, he thinks—and he addresses the niceties of helping a friend in need. He concludes book 9 with a focus on the shared activities that fill the lives of good people who are friends with each other.

[10.1]. Μετὰ δὲ ταῦτα περὶ ἡδονῆς ἴσως ἕπεται διελθεῖν. μάλιστα γὰρ δοκεῖ συνῳκειῶσθαι τῷ γένει
ἡμῶν, διὸ παιδεύουσι τοὺς νέους οἰακίζοντες
ἡδονῇ καὶ λύπῃ· δοκεῖ δὲ καὶ πρὸς τὴν τοῦ ἤθους
ἀρετὴν μέγιστον εἶναι τὸ χαίρειν οἷς δεῖ καὶ μισεῖν
ἃ δεῖ. διατείνει γὰρ ταῦτα διὰ παντὸς τοῦ βίου,
ῥοπὴν ἔχοντα καὶ δύναμιν πρὸς ἀρετήν τε καὶ
τὸν εὐδαίμονα βίον· . . .

8. HOW WE FLOURISH

(Book 10)
In book 10 Aristotle returns to the topic of happiness and seeks to identify the activity in which it consists. In the first six chapters he considers the nature and value of pleasure.

Pleasure

[10.1] Our next task, presumably, is to discuss pleasure. After all, it seems to be bound up with the kind of creature we are (which is why educators try to steer young people by using pleasure and pain). It also seems crucial for virtue of character that we take pleasure in and dislike the right things. Our whole life is pervaded by these feelings, and they have powerful influence on our prospects for virtue and a happy life. . . .

[10.4] Τί δ' ἐστὶν ἢ ποῖόν τι, καταφανέστερον γέ-
νοιτ' ἂν ἀπ' ἀρχῆς ἀναλαβοῦσιν. δοκεῖ γὰρ ἡ μὲν
ὅρασις καθ' ὁντινοῦν χρόνον τελεία εἶναι· οὐ γάρ
ἐστιν ἐνδεὴς οὐδενὸς ὃ εἰς ὕστερον γινόμενον τε-
λειώσει αὐτῆς τὸ εἶδος· τοιούτῳ δ' ἔοικε καὶ ἡ
ἡδονή. ὅλον γάρ τι ἐστί, . . .

κατὰ πᾶσαν γὰρ αἴσθησίν ἐστιν ἡδονή, ὁμοίως
δὲ καὶ διάνοιαν καὶ θεωρίαν, ἡδίστη δ' ἡ τελειοτάτη, τελειοτάτη δ' ἡ τοῦ εὖ ἔχοντος πρὸς τὸ
σπουδαιότατον τῶν ὑπ' αὐτήν· τελειοῖ δὲ τὴν
ἐνέργειαν ἡ ἡδονή. . . . οὐχ ὡς ἡ ἕξις ἐνυπάρ-
χουσα, ἀλλ' ὡς ἐπιγινόμενόν τι τέλος, οἷον τοῖς ἀκ-
μαίοις ἡ ὥρα. ἕως ἂν οὖν τό τε νοητὸν ἢ αἰσθητὸν

Over chapters 1–3, Aristotle surveys some of his contemporaries' views about pleasure. In chapter 4, he gives his own view.

[10.4] We can clarify what pleasure is, or what sort of thing it is, if we start with sight as an example. The activity of seeing is complete over any interval of time; nothing needs to happen later for it to completely realize its form. Pleasure is like that, since it is something whole. . . .

We get pleasure from every sense, and likewise from intellect and theoretical thought. The most pleasant activity is the most perfectly realized, and this comes from a faculty in good shape that is dealing with the most excellent objects that fall under it. The pleasure makes the activity perfect . . . —but not in the way the disposition present in the subject makes the activity perfect; pleasure is a finishing touch, like full bloom in the prime of life. As long as the object of thought or of sense is as it should be, and also

ἢ οἷον δεῖ καὶ τὸ κρῖνον ἢ θεωροῦν, ἔσται ἐν τῇ
ἐνεργείᾳ ἡ ἡδονή· . . .

συνεζεῦχθαι μὲν γὰρ ταῦτα φαίνεται καὶ χωρι-
σμὸν οὐ δέχεσθαι· ἄνευ τε γὰρ ἐνεργείας οὐ γίνεται ἡδονή, πᾶσάν τε ἐνέργειαν τελειοῖ ἡ ἡδονή.

[10.6] Εἰρημένων δὲ τῶν περὶ τὰς ἀρετάς τε καὶ
φιλίας καὶ ἡδονάς, λοιπὸν περὶ εὐδαιμονίας
τύπῳ διελθεῖν, ἐπειδὴ τέλος αὐτὴν τίθεμεν τῶν
ἀνθρωπίνων. ἀναλαβοῦσι δὴ τὰ προειρημένα συν-
τομώτερος ἂν εἴη ὁ λόγος. . . . εἰ δὴ . . . εἰς ἐνέργειάν τινα θετέον, . . . τῶν δ' ἐνεργειῶν αἳ μέν
εἰσιν ἀναγκαῖαι καὶ δι' ἕτερα αἱρεταὶ αἳ δὲ καθ'
αὑτάς, δῆλον ὅτι τὴν εὐδαιμονίαν τῶν καθ' αὑτὰς

the faculty that judges or thinks, there will be pleasure in the activity. . . .

Pleasure seems to be inextricably bound up with being alive: without activity there is no pleasure, and every activity is perfectly completed by pleasure.

Chapter 5 explores further implications of the tight connection between pleasure and activity and concludes Aristotle's account of pleasure. In chapter 6 he resumes his original inquiry into happiness.

[10.6] Now that we have discussed the virtues, friendship, and pleasures, our remaining task is to delineate happiness, since we take it to be the goal of humans. We can shorten our discussion by relying on our prior remarks. . . . If . . . we must take happiness to be an activity . . . and if some activities are necessary for a further goal, while others are for their own sakes, then clearly we must take happiness to be an activity chosen for its own sake and not for the sake of something

αἱρετῶν τινὰ θετέον καὶ οὐ τῶν δι᾽ ἄλλο· οὐδενὸς
γὰρ ἐνδεὴς ἡ εὐδαιμονία ἀλλ᾽ αὐτάρκης. . . .

[10.7] Εἰ δ᾽ ἐστὶν ἡ εὐδαιμονία κατ᾽ ἀρετὴν ἐνέργεια, εὔλογον κατὰ τὴν κρατίστην· αὕτη δ᾽ ἂν εἴη
τοῦ ἀρίστου. εἴτε δὴ νοῦς τοῦτο εἴτε ἄλλο τι, ὃ δὴ
κατὰ φύσιν δοκεῖ ἄρχειν καὶ ἡγεῖσθαι καὶ ἔννοιαν
ἔχειν περὶ καλῶν καὶ θείων, εἴτε θεῖον ὂν καὶ αὐτὸ
εἴτε τῶν ἐν ἡμῖν τὸ θειότατον, ἡ τούτου ἐνέργεια

else. After all, happiness lacks nothing; it is self-sufficient. . . .

The rest of chapter 6 rejects the proposal that recreation or leisure meets this criterion for happiness. Chapter 7 returns to the big question left open in book 1 when Aristotle identified happiness as activity of "the best and most complete virtue" [1.7]. Aristotle now asks what kind of virtue is "the best and most complete"? He surprises many readers by claiming that it is virtue of the theoretical (or "scientific") part of the soul.

LIFE OF THE MIND

[10.7] If happiness is activity that comes from virtue, it makes sense that the virtue in question must be the highest, which would be the virtue of our best part. Whether that is intellect (or something else that seems to be our natural ruler and leader, and understands objects that are noble and divine), and whether it is divine itself

κατὰ τὴν οἰκείαν ἀρετὴν εἴη ἂν ἡ τελεία εὐδαιμονία. ὅτι δ' ἐστὶ θεωρητική, εἴρηται. . . . κρατίστη
τε γὰρ αὕτη ἐστὶν ἡ ἐνέργεια (καὶ γὰρ ὁ νοῦς τῶν
ἐν ἡμῖν, καὶ τῶν γνωστῶν, περὶ ἃ ὁ νοῦς)· . . .

οἰόμεθά τε δεῖν ἡδονὴν παραμεμῖχθαι τῇ εὐδαιμο-
νίᾳ, ἡδίστη δὲ τῶν κατ' ἀρετὴν ἐνεργειῶν ἡ κατὰ
τὴν σοφίαν ὁμολογουμένως ἐστίν· δοκεῖ γοῦν ἡ
φιλοσοφία θαυμαστὰς ἡδονὰς ἔχειν καθαρειότητι

(or the most divine thing inside us), it is activity *of this*, performed with the virtue proper to it, that would be perfect happiness. We have already said that this activity is *theoretical thinking*. . . . It is our highest activity because intellect is our highest faculty, and its objects are the highest objects of knowledge. . . .

Aristotle next enumerates various features of happiness and argues that each is manifested more fully when we engage in "theoretical thinking" than when we exercise the virtues of character. His emphasis is on the requirement—originally stated in [1.7] and repeated in [10.6]—that happiness is chosen for its own sake, and not for the sake of anything else.

We think happiness must have pleasure mixed into it, and it is generally agreed that the activity of *scientific learning* is the most pleasant virtuous activity. The pleasures of philosophy, I would venture, are marvelously pure and stable,

καὶ τῷ βεβαίῳ, εὔλογον δὲ τοῖς εἰδόσι τῶν ζητούν-
των ἡδίω τὴν διαγωγὴν εἶναι. . . .

δόξαι τ᾽ ἂν αὐτὴ μόνη δι᾽ αὑτὴν ἀγαπᾶσθαι·
οὐδὲν γὰρ ἀπ᾽ αὐτῆς γίνεται παρὰ τὸ θεωρῆσαι,
ἀπὸ δὲ τῶν πρακτικῶν ἢ πλεῖον ἢ ἔλαττον περι-
ποιούμεθα παρὰ τὴν πρᾶξιν. δοκεῖ τε ἡ εὐδαιμονία ἐν τῇ σχολῇ εἶναι· ἀσχολούμεθα γὰρ ἵνα
σχολάζωμεν, καὶ πολεμοῦμεν ἵν᾽ εἰρήνην ἄγω-
μεν. τῶν μὲν οὖν πρακτικῶν ἀρετῶν ἐν τοῖς πολι-
τικοῖς ἢ ἐν τοῖς πολεμικοῖς ἡ ἐνέργεια, αἱ δὲ περὶ
ταῦτα πράξεις δοκοῦσιν ἄσχολοι εἶναι, αἱ μὲν
πολεμικαὶ καὶ παντελῶς (οὐδεὶς γὰρ αἱρεῖται τὸ
πολεμεῖν τοῦ πολεμεῖν ἕνεκα, οὐδὲ παρασκευάζει
πόλεμον· δόξαι γὰρ ἂν παντελῶς μιαιφόνος τις
εἶναι, εἰ τοὺς φίλους πολεμίους ποιοῖτο, ἵνα
μάχαι καὶ φόνοι γίνοιντο)·

ἔστι δὲ καὶ ἡ τοῦ πολιτικοῦ ἄσχολος, καὶ παρ᾽
αὐτὸ τὸ πολιτεύεσθαι περιποιουμένη δυναστείας καὶ τιμὰς ἢ τήν γε εὐδαιμονίαν αὑτῷ καὶ

and it is a more pleasant pastime if you have learned it than if you are still seeking it. . . .

It would seem that theoretical thinking on its own is cherished for what it is. After all, we get nothing from it beyond the act of thinking, while when we perform *actions* we get something beyond the action, to one degree or another. Also, happiness seems to involve leisure: we busy ourselves with work in order to have leisure, and we go to war in order to have peace. Now, we exercise the action-oriented virtues in the political arena or on the battlefield, where we are hardly at leisure, least of all on the battlefield. (No one chooses to go to war for its own sake, or starts a war simply to have one; someone who made enemies of their friends in order to have battles and slaughter would strike us as utterly murderous.)

There is no leisure in the political life, either, and beyond the political activity itself, it gets you power and honor, or at least happiness for yourself and the citizens. That is something

τοῖς πολίταις, ἑτέραν οὖσαν τῆς πολιτικῆς, ἣν καὶ
ζητοῦμεν δῆλον ὡς ἑτέραν οὖσαν.

εἰ δὴ τῶν μὲν κατὰ τὰς ἀρετὰς πράξεων αἱ πο-
λιτικαὶ καὶ πολεμικαὶ κάλλει καὶ μεγέθει προέχου-
σιν, αὗται δ᾽ ἄσχολοι καὶ τέλους τινὸς ἐφίενται
καὶ οὐ δι᾽ αὑτὰς αἱρεταί εἰσιν, ἡ δὲ τοῦ νοῦ ἐνέργεια σπουδῇ τε διαφέρειν δοκεῖ θεωρητικὴ οὖσα,
καὶ παρ᾽ αὑτὴν οὐδενὸς ἐφίεσθαι τέλους, καὶ ἔχειν
τὴν ἡδονὴν οἰκείαν (αὕτη δὲ συναύξει τὴν ἐνέργειαν), καὶ τὸ αὔταρκες δὴ καὶ σχολαστικὸν καὶ
ἄτρυτον ὡς ἀνθρώπῳ, καὶ ὅσα ἄλλα τῷ μακαρίῳ
ἀπονέμεται, τὰ κατὰ ταύτην τὴν ἐνέργειαν φαίνεται ὄντα· ἡ τελεία δὴ εὐδαιμονία αὕτη ἂν εἴη ἀνθρώπου, λαβοῦσα μῆκος βίου τέλειον· οὐδὲν γὰρ
ἀτελές ἐστι τῶν τῆς εὐδαιμονίας.

ὁ δὲ τοιοῦτος ἂν εἴη βίος κρείττων ἢ κατ᾽ ἄν-
θρωπον· οὐ γὰρ ᾗ ἄνθρωπός ἐστιν οὕτω βιώσε-
ται, ἀλλ᾽ ᾗ θεῖόν τι ἐν αὐτῷ ὑπάρχει· ὅσον δὲ

distinct from the political activity itself, and we clearly pursue it as a distinct objective.

Virtuous actions in politics and war do stand out in their splendor and importance—but they deprive us of leisure, they are goal directed, and they are not chosen because of themselves. Activity of intellect, on the other hand, seems to be exceptionally serious (since it is theoretical) and to be directed at no goal beyond itself. It seems to have its own proper pleasure—which enhances the activity—and to be as self-sufficient, leisured, and weariless as is possible for a human being. Every other feature attributed to a blessedly happy person clearly comes from its activity. So that activity would be the perfect happiness of a human being—provided it lasts for a complete life, since nothing about happiness is incomplete.

Such a life would be higher than a life lived on human terms, since we live in this way not insofar as we are human, but insofar as there is something divine in us. To the extent that this

διαφέρει τοῦτο τοῦ συνθέτου, τοσοῦτον καὶ ἡ
ἐνέργεια τῆς κατὰ τὴν ἄλλην ἀρετήν. εἰ δὴ θεῖον
ὁ νοῦς πρὸς τὸν ἄνθρωπον, καὶ ὁ κατὰ τοῦτον
βίος θεῖος πρὸς τὸν ἀνθρώπινον βίον. οὐ χρὴ δὲ
κατὰ τοὺς παραινοῦντας ἀνθρώπινα φρονεῖν ἄνθρωπον ὄντα οὐδὲ θνητὰ τὸν θνητόν, ἀλλ' ἐφ'
ὅσον ἐνδέχεται ἀθανατίζειν καὶ πάντα ποιεῖν πρὸς
τὸ ζῆν κατὰ τὸ κράτιστον τῶν ἐν αὑτῷ· εἰ γὰρ καὶ
τῷ ὄγκῳ μικρόν ἐστι, δυνάμει καὶ τιμιότητι πολὺ
μᾶλλον πάντων ὑπερέχει.

δόξειε δ' ἂν καὶ εἶναι ἕκαστος τοῦτο, εἴπερ τὸ
κύριον καὶ ἄμεινον. ἄτοπον οὖν γίνοιτ' ἄν, εἰ μὴ
τὸν αὑτοῦ βίον αἱροῖτο ἀλλά τινος ἄλλου. τὸ λε-
χθέν τε πρότερον ἁρμόσει καὶ νῦν· τὸ γὰρ οἰκεῖον
ἑκάστῳ τῇ φύσει κράτιστον καὶ ἥδιστόν ἐστιν
ἑκάστῳ· καὶ τῷ ἀνθρώπῳ δὴ ὁ κατὰ τὸν νοῦν

divine element is superior to the composite, its activity is superior to that of the rest of virtue. So if intellect is divine in comparison to a human being, the life of intellect is divine in comparison to a human life. But there is no requirement to heed the proverbial advice that a human should think human thoughts, and a mortal, mortal thoughts. Rather, we should exercise our immortality as far as this is possible and do all we can to live by the highest part of ourselves. Although it is small in size, its power and dignity surpass all else.

This would seem to be what each person actually is, given that it is supreme in us and our better part. It certainly would be strange to choose a life that is not our own but belongs to something else. And what we said earlier fits with what we are saying now, since what naturally belongs to something is best and most pleasant for it. In the case of a human being, that is a life of intellect—inasmuch as that is what a

βίος, εἴπερ τοῦτο μάλιστα ἄνθρωπος. οὗτος ἄρα καὶ εὐδαιμονέστατος.

[10.8] Δευτέρως δ' ὁ κατὰ τὴν ἄλλην ἀρετήν· αἱ γὰρ κατὰ ταύτην ἐνέργειαι ἀνθρωπικαί. δίκαια γὰρ καὶ ἀνδρεῖα καὶ τὰ ἄλλα τὰ κατὰ τὰς ἀρετὰς πρὸς ἀλλήλους πράττομεν ἐν συναλλάγμασι καὶ χρείαις καὶ πράξεσι παντοίαις ἔν τε τοῖς πάθεσι διατηροῦντες τὸ πρέπον ἑκάστῳ· ταῦτα δ' εἶναι φαίνεται πάντα ἀνθρωπικά.

ἔνια δὲ καὶ συμβαίνειν ἀπὸ τοῦ σώματος δοκεῖ, καὶ πολλὰ συνῳκειῶσθαι τοῖς πάθεσιν ἡ τοῦ ἤθους ἀρετή. συνέζευκται δὲ καὶ ἡ φρόνησις τῇ τοῦ ἤθους ἀρετῇ, καὶ αὕτη τῇ φρονήσει, εἴπερ αἱ μὲν τῆς φρονήσεως ἀρχαὶ κατὰ τὰς ἠθικάς εἰσιν ἀρετάς, τὸ δ' ὀρθὸν τῶν ἠθικῶν κατὰ τὴν φρόνη-σιν. συνηρτημέναι δ' αὗται καὶ τοῖς πάθεσι περὶ τὸ σύνθετον ἂν εἶεν· αἱ δὲ τοῦ συνθέτου ἀρεταὶ

human being *is* most of all. So that life is the happiest.

Human and Godlike Happiness

[10.8] Second happiest will be the life that exercises the rest of virtue. Its activities, after all, are in the human domain. It is *to each another* that we practice justice, for example, or bravery or other virtuous actions—giving each person what is due to them in contracts, in business, in actions of all types, and in our feelings as well. All that appears to be entirely human.

It seems some of it also arises from the body, with multiple connections binding virtue of character to our feelings. Good judgment is yoked to virtue of character, and virtue of character to it, inasmuch as good judgment gets its principles from the character virtues, and they get their correctness from it. Since these virtues are bound together with our feelings, they pertain to the composite.[30] Thus they are in the

ἀνθρωπικαί· καὶ ὁ βίος δὴ ὁ κατὰ ταύτας καὶ ἡ εὐδαιμονία. ἡ δὲ τοῦ νοῦ κεχωρισμένη· . . .

τοὺς θεοὺς γὰρ μάλιστα ὑπειλήφαμεν μακαρίους καὶ εὐδαίμονας εἶναι· πράξεις δὲ ποίας ἀπονεῖμαι χρεὼν αὐτοῖς; πότερα τὰς δικαίας; ἢ γελοῖοι φανοῦνται συναλλάττοντες καὶ παρακαταθήκας ἀποδιδόντες καὶ ὅσα τοιαῦτα; ἀλλὰ τὰς ἀνδρείους ** ὑπομένοντας τὰ φοβερὰ καὶ κινδυνεύοντας ὅτι καλόν; ἢ τὰς ἐλευθερίους; τίνι δὲ δώσουσιν; ἄτοπον δ' εἰ καὶ ἔσται αὐτοῖς νόμισμα ἤ τι τοιοῦτον. αἱ δὲ σώφρονες τί ἂν εἶεν; ἢ φορτικὸς ὁ ἔπαινος, ὅτι οὐκ ἔχουσι φαύλας ἐπιθυμίας; διεξιοῦσι δὲ πάντα φαίνοιτ' ἂν τὰ περὶ τὰς πράξεις μικρὰ καὶ

human domain, and so is the life and happiness that comes from them. The life of the intellect, on the other hand, is separate. . . .

Aristotle next claims that the godlike life of intellect is less dependent on external resources than the more human life of virtuous character. Then he invokes theological considerations to support his conclusion that the life of intellect is happier.

We consider the gods to be supremely blessed and happy, but what sorts of actions should we attribute to them? Just acts? Wouldn't they be ridiculous making contracts, returning deposits, and doing other such things? Brave acts? Shall we say they withstand terrifying situations and risk dangers because it is noble to do so? Generous acts? To whom will they give? It would be strange for them to have such things as money. And how could they act with self-control? Surely it is crude to praise them for not having bad desires. To anyone who considers

ἀνάξια θεῶν. ἀλλὰ μὴν ζῆν γε πάντες ὑπειλήφα-
σιν αὐτοὺς καὶ ἐνεργεῖν ἄρα· οὐ γὰρ δὴ καθεύδειν
ὥσπερ τὸν Ἐνδυμίωνα. τῷ δὴ ζῶντι τοῦ πράττειν
ἀφαιρουμένου, ἔτι δὲ μᾶλλον τοῦ ποιεῖν, τί λείπεται πλὴν θεωρία; ὥστε ἡ τοῦ θεοῦ ἐνέργεια,
μακαριότητι διαφέρουσα, θεωρητικὴ ἂν εἴη·
καὶ τῶν ἀνθρωπίνων δὴ ἡ ταύτη συγγενεστάτη
εὐδαιμονικωτάτη . . .

Δεήσει δὲ καὶ τῆς ἐκτὸς εὐημερίας ἀνθρώπῳ ὄντι·
οὐ γὰρ αὐτάρκης ἡ φύσις πρὸς τὸ θεωρεῖν, ἀλλὰ
δεῖ καὶ τὸ σῶμα ὑγιαίνειν καὶ τροφὴν καὶ τὴν
λοιπὴν θεραπείαν ὑπάρχειν. οὐ μὴν οἰητέον γε

the matter carefully, it is clear that everything to do with actions is trifling and unworthy of the gods. Still, everyone agrees that the gods are alive and active—not asleep like Endymion.[31] But once we have eliminated action from their life—and production too, all the more—what activity is left except theoretical thinking? The result is that the activity of god, exceptional in its blessedness, is theoretical thinking, and the human activity most akin to it will make us happiest. . . .

Aristotle draws the further inference that non-human animals are incapable of happiness, since they are incapable of theoretical thinking. He then focuses on the external conditions necessary for human happiness.
Being human, we will also need some external prosperity. That's because our nature is not sufficient on its own for theoretical thinking; we need a healthy body along with food and other forms of sustenance. Still, even if we can't be

πολλῶν καὶ μεγάλων δεήσεσθαι τὸν εὐδαιμονή-
σοντα, εἰ μὴ ἐνδέχεται ἄνευ τῶν ἐκτὸς ἀγαθῶν
μακάριον εἶναι· οὐ γὰρ ἐν τῇ ὑπερβολῇ τὸ αὔταρκες οὐδ᾽ ἡ πρᾶξις, δυνατὸν δὲ καὶ μὴ ἄρχοντα
γῆς καὶ θαλάττης πράττειν τὰ καλά· καὶ γὰρ ἀπὸ
μετρίων δύναιτ᾽ ἄν τις πράττειν κατὰ τὴν ἀρετήν. . . . καὶ Σόλων δὲ τοὺς εὐδαίμονας ἴσως
ἀπεφαίνετο καλῶς, εἰπὼν μετρίως τοῖς ἐκτὸς
κεχορηγημένους, πεπραγότας δὲ τὰ κάλλισθ᾽, ὡς
ᾤετο, καὶ βεβιωκότας σωφρόνως· . . .

ὁ δὲ κατὰ νοῦν ἐνεργῶν καὶ τοῦτον θεραπεύων
καὶ διακείμενος ἄριστα καὶ θεοφιλέστατος ἔοικεν.
εἰ γάρ τις ἐπιμέλεια τῶν ἀνθρωπίνων ὑπὸ θεῶν
γίνεται, ὥσπερ δοκεῖ, καὶ εἴη ἂν εὔλογον χαίρειν
τε αὐτοὺς τῷ ἀρίστῳ καὶ συγγενεστάτῳ (τοῦτο
δ᾽ ἂν εἴη ὁ νοῦς) καὶ τοὺς ἀγαπῶντας μάλιστα
τοῦτο καὶ τιμῶντας ἀντευποιεῖν ὡς τῶν φίλων
αὐτοῖς ἐπιμελουμένους καὶ ὀρθῶς τε καὶ καλῶς
πράττοντας. ὅτι δὲ πάντα ταῦτα τῷ σοφῷ μάλισθ᾽

happy *without* external goods, it is wrong to think that we need a great number or quantity of them to be happy. Self-sufficiency does not require excess; and action doesn't either. You can perform noble actions even if you do not rule over earth and sea, and you can practice virtue even with moderate resources. . . . Presumably Solon was right to define happy people as those who had moderate resources, performed . . . the finest actions, and practiced self-control throughout their lives. . . .

It seems that people who exercise their intellect and look after it are in the best condition and most beloved by the gods. If the gods care at all about human affairs, as it seems they do, it would make sense for them to rejoice in what is best and most akin to themselves (that is, intellect) and to reward the people who cherish and honor it most highly—in recognition that such people, as stewards of what the gods themselves hold dear, act rightly and well. It is not hard to see that all these features belong

ὑπάρχει, οὐκ ἄδηλον. θεοφιλέστατος ἄρα. τὸν αὐτὸν δ' εἰκὸς καὶ εὐδαιμονέστατον· ...

[10.9] Ἆρ' οὖν εἰ περί τε τούτων καὶ τῶν ἀρετῶν, ἔτι δὲ καὶ φιλίας καὶ ἡδονῆς, ἱκανῶς εἴρηται τοῖς τύποις, τέλος ἔχειν οἰητέον τὴν προαίρεσιν; ἢ καθάπερ λέγεται, οὐκ ἔστιν ἐν τοῖς πρακτοῖς τέλος τὸ θεωρῆσαι ἕκαστα καὶ γνῶναι, ἀλλὰ μᾶλλον τὸ πράττειν αὐτά· ...

especially to people who are *learned in science*. So it would seem that those people would be most beloved by the gods, and the happiest. . . .

[10.9] Well, if we have given an adequate sketch of happiness and virtue, as well as friendship and pleasure, have we accomplished what we intended? Or is it rather that—as the saying goes—when we investigate what is to be done, our goal is not simply to theorize and learn what to do, but to do it? . . .

In this closing chapter of the NICOMACHEAN ETHICS, *Aristotle proceeds to ask about the political and social conditions in which human happiness will be realized. These questions introduce the subject of the* POLITICS, *to which this chapter explicitly serves as a preface.*

APPENDIX: THE HUMAN SOUL
AND ITS VIRTUES

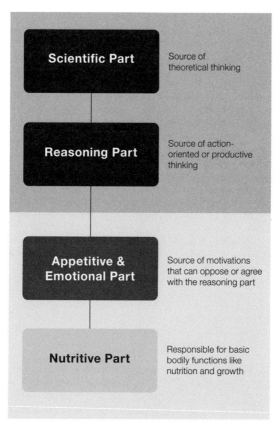

Figure 1. Parts of the soul

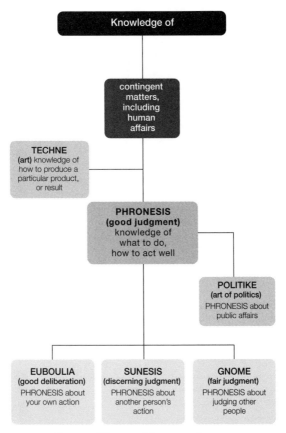

Figure 2. Virtues of the reasoning part

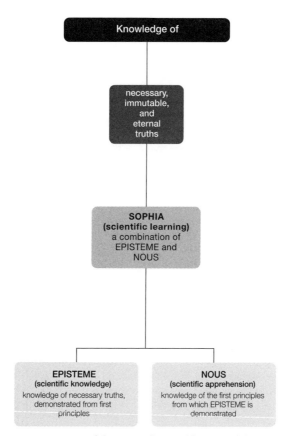

Figure 3. Virtues of the scientific part (theoretical thought)

Figure 4. Some virtues of character

NOTES

1. Aristotle's own position is that a life of eudaimonia contains many pleasures, but what makes it *eudaimōn* is not pleasure but virtue. Among later philosophers, Epicureans identified eudaimonia with pleasure, while some Stoics denied that pleasure was necessary for eudaimonia.

2. "happy, adj. and n., A.I.1–2," *OED Online*, Oxford University Press, June 2021, accessed August 2, 2021.

3. Cicero in the first century BCE credits Aristotle with a "golden flow" of words (*Academica* 2.119). Porphyry in the third century CE reports that Andronicus "divided Aristotle's writings into treatises by collecting related materials together" (*Vita Plotini* 24.7–11).

4. When Aristotle asks this question in Greek, he asks about the *ergon* of a human being. The

term *ergon* is sometimes translated "function" (and I have retained that translation in the heading, so that readers can find this famous argument) but that translation is misleading to the extent that it suggests Aristotle thinks humans are created for a particular purpose, or have a role in a larger cosmic system. For Aristotle, the human ergon is simply activity characteristic of human beings.

5. The kithara is a multistringed instrument from which the modern guitar gets its name.

6. In the legends about Troy, Priam reigned as king during the height of the city's powers, but in his old age the city was sacked, his children were killed, and he died a humiliating death.

7. Solon was an Athenian lawmaker and poet active in the early sixth century BCE.

8. Aristotle makes a philosophical distinction between exercising self-control (*enkrateia*)—doing the right thing after winning an internal struggle against the impulse to do otherwise—and having self-discipline (*sōphrosunē*). A person with self-discipline sees what they should

do, does it without struggle or ambivalence, and acts from a trained and stable disposition to respond in this way.

9. Milo of Croton, a champion wrestler at multiple Olympic games in the sixth century BCE, was legendary for his feats of strength and for the amount of food he consumed while training. A daily diet of ten minae would be about ten pounds of food.

10. Aristotle remarks that "art imitates nature" in *Physics* 2.2 (194a21–22).

11. A more literal translation of Aristotle's name for this virtue is "magnificence" (*megaloprepeia*). Very wealthy citizens in Athens were expected to make large expenditures on behalf of the city (such as equipping a warship) or to pay for public entertainments (such as dramatic festivals), or to host large feasts. These activities overlap with the domain of what we call *philanthropy* today.

12. Homer, *Odyssey* 12.108–10, 219–20. Odysseus must pilot his ship between two hazards: a whirlpool that will sink the ship and a monster

who will snatch sailors from the ship if it sails within reach. He is advised to steer away from the whirlpool ("surge and spray") because losing the entire ship and crew would be worse than losing some of the crew but saving the ship.

13. In Homer's *Iliad* 3.159–60, the elders of Troy say of Helen, whose beauty they blame for starting the Trojan war: "let her go away in the ships . . . lest she be . . . a grief to us and our children" (trans. R. Lattimore [Chicago: University of Chicago Press, 1951]).

14. Aristotle sometimes explains human action as based on an argument with one premise that states a general action-guiding principle (e.g., "We should avoid eating sweets") and another premise about the particular circumstances ("this food is sweet"). He calls the general principle a "universal belief" in 7.3 (1147a25).

15. In a scene from Euripides's lost tragedy *Cresphontes*, Queen Merope kills a man she believes to have murdered her son, unaware that he is her long-lost son in disguise.

16. Aristotle has Plato in mind here. A regular refrain in Plato's dialogues is that vice and wrongdoing are involuntary: *Protagoras* 345e; *Gorgias* 509e; *Timaeus* 86e; *Laws* 731c, 734b, 860d–e.

17. During the Corinthian war of 395–386 BCE, Sparta and Argos were opponents. In one battle, a contingent of Spartans took up the shields of their allies from Sicyon, who had suffered heavy losses; the Argives attacked the disguised Spartans, expecting they would be easy to defeat (Xenophon, *Hellenica* 4.4.10).

18. These are what we might describe as mental pleasures.

19. Aristotle has in mind terms like "money lover" (*philochrēmatos*), "honor lover" (*philotimos*), or "crazy about horses" (*philippos*).

20. Aristotle calls this virtue *philia* in 2.7 (where it is translated "friendliness"). It is, however, the same term he uses for friendship in books 8–9.

21. In Plato's *Republic* the three parts of the soul are the appetitive, the spirited, and the reasoning (*logistikon*) part (439d–e).

22. When Aristotle describes some thinking as "theoretical," he does not mean "speculative"; he means that the sole aim of such thinking is to grasp the truth—in contrast to action-oriented or productive thinking, which has the further aim of issuing in action or bringing about results in the world.

23. Aristotle defines demonstration (*apodeixis*) as the kind of deduction (*sullogismos*) that yields scientific knowledge (*Posterior Analytics* 1.2).

24. Aristotle defines nature as an internal principle of change (*Physics* 2.1). Artefacts such as tables and chairs are produced by something external to them (i.e., a carpenter)—unlike natural things such as plants and animals, which grow from an internal principle.

25. Pericles (495–429 BCE) was a political leader and general in Athens during the height of that city's economic and military dominance.

26. Anaximander and Thales were Milesian cosmologists active in the sixth century BCE. Plato reports a story that Thales, while making astronomical observations, fell into a ditch because he

was looking at the sky rather than at his feet (*Theaetetus* 174a).

27. The self-indulgent (*akolastos*) person has a vice of character and pursues bad pleasures without ambivalence. The person with *akrasia*, by contrast, struggles against giving in to the attraction.

28. Empedocles of Acragas was a fifth-century philosopher who wrote in verse.

29. The quoted phrase is spoken by the Homeric hero Diomedes (*Iliad* 10.224) as he seeks a partner to accompany him on a dangerous mission. Plato and Aristotle each quote this phrase twice.

30. That is, a composite of body and soul.

31. In the various versions of the myth of Endymion, the young man is cast into a perpetual sleep by the gods, thereby achieving immortality and eternal youth.

TEXTUAL NOTES

1. 1126b30 I retain Bywater's reading and reject Rackham's replacement of μὴ by ἢ (*Loeb Classical Library*), which is the reading translated by Urmson in the *Revised Oxford Translation*.

2. 1140b21 ἀληθῆ (Bywater) >> ἀληθοῦς (Mᵇ Γ).

3. 1144a26 αὐτοῦ (Bywater) >> αὐτῶν (MSS).

KEY ARISTOTELIAN TERMS

Brief explanations are to be found on the pages indicated.

akolasia	self-indulgence (a vice, opposite to *sōphrosunē*)	287n27
akrasia	losing control (opposite to *enkrateia*)	215, 287n27
aretē	virtue	23, 49, 278–280
enkrateia	controlling yourself (not a virtue; opposite to *akrasia*)	215, 282n8
epistēmē	science	177–179, 279
ergon	activity or product (*not* function)	17, 281n4
eudaimonia	happiness	xiii, 17, 255
kalon	noble, decent, splendid, fine, honorable	101
phusis	nature	283n10, 286n24
psuchē	soul	21, 277

FURTHER READING

Emphasis is on works that are aimed at the general reader.

TRANSLATIONS INTO ENGLISH OF THE ENTIRE *NICOMACHEAN ETHICS*

Beresford's translation is the most colloquial; Rowe's is exemplary in capturing elements of Aristotle's style while still remaining highly readable.

Beresford, A., trans. 2020. *Aristotle: The Nicomachean Ethics*. Penguin Classics. New York: Random House.

Broadie, S., and C. Rowe. 2002. *Aristotle: Nicomachean Ethics*. Translated with historical introduction by Christopher Rowe. Philosophical introduction and commentary by Sarah Broadie. Oxford: Oxford University Press.

Crisp, R., trans. 2000. *Aristotle: Nicomachean Ethics*.
Cambridge Texts in the History of Philosophy.
Cambridge: Cambridge University Press.

Irwin, T. H., trans. 2019. *Aristotle: Nicomachean Ethics*. With introduction, notes, and glossary.
3rd ed. Indianapolis: Hackett.

Reeve, C.D.C., trans. 2014. *Aristotle: Nicomachean Ethics*. With introduction and notes. Indianapolis: Hackett.

Ross, D., and L. Brown. 2009. *Aristotle: The Nicomachean Ethics*. Translated by David Ross (1925). Revised with an introduction and notes by Lesley Brown. Oxford World's Classics. Oxford: Oxford University Press.

Translations of Other Aristotelian Works

Barnes, J., ed. 1984. *The Complete Works of Aristotle: The Revised Oxford Translation*. 2 vols. Princeton, NJ: Princeton University Press.

Irwin, T. and G. Fine, trans. 1995. *Aristotle: Selections*. Translated with introduction, notes, and glossary. Indianapolis: Hackett.

FURTHER READING

ARISTOTLE'S HISTORICAL, POLITICAL, AND SOCIAL CONTEXT

Dover, K. 1974. *Greek Popular Morality in the Time of Plato and Aristotle*. Indianapolis: Hackett.

Rhodes, P. J. 2006. *A History of the Classical Greek World 478–323*. Oxford: Blackwell.

ARISTOTLE'S LIFE, WORKS, AND SCHOOL

Adamson, P. 2015. "Lost and Found: Aristotelianism after Aristotle." In *Philosophy in the Hellenistic and Roman Worlds: The History of Philosophy without Any Gaps*, 2:174–80. Oxford: Oxford University Press.

Hatzimichali, M. 2016. "Andronicus of Rhodes and the Construction of the Corpus Aristotelicum." In *Brill's Companion to the Reception of Aristotle in Antiquity*, edited by A. Falcon, 81–100. Leiden: Brill.

Natali, C. 2013. *Aristotle: His Life and School*. Edited by D. S. Hutchinson. Princeton, NJ: Princeton University Press.

Overviews of Aristotle's Ethics

See also the introductions and notes in the translations listed above.

Garver, E. 2006. *Confronting Aristotle's Ethics: Ancient and Modern Morality*. Chicago: University of Chicago Press.

Gottlieb, P. 2022. *Aristotle's Ethics: Nicomachean and Eudemian Themes*. Cambridge Elements in Ethics. Cambridge: Cambridge University Press.

Kraut, R. "Aristotle's Ethics." In *The Stanford Encyclopedia of Philosophy*. Summer 2018 ed., edited by Edward N. Zalta, https://plato .stanford.edu/archives/sum2018/entries/aristotle -ethics/.

Meyer, S. S. 2008. "Aristotle and the Pursuit of Happiness." In *Ancient Ethics: A Critical Introduction*, 50–94. New York: Routledge.

Pakaluk, M. 2005. *Aristotle's Nicomachean Ethics: An Introduction*. Cambridge: Cambridge University Press.

FURTHER READING

COLLECTIONS OF ESSAYS ON VARIOUS TOPICS IN ARISTOTLE'S ETHICS

Kraut, R., ed. 2006. *The Blackwell Guide to Aristotle's Ethics*. Oxford: Blackwell.

Miller, J., ed. 2011. *Aristotle's Nicomachean Ethics: A Critical Guide*. Cambridge: Cambridge University Press.

Polansky, Ronald, ed. 2014. *The Cambridge Companion to Aristotle's Nicomachean Ethics*. Cambridge: Cambridge University Press.

Rorty, A. O., ed. 1980. *Essays on Aristotle's Ethics*. Berkeley: University of California Press.

INDEX OF PASSAGES TRANSLATED

Chapters divisions are from Bywater; most passages have ellipses.

INDEX OF PASSAGES TRANSLATED